MW01410595

A School Lunch Revolution

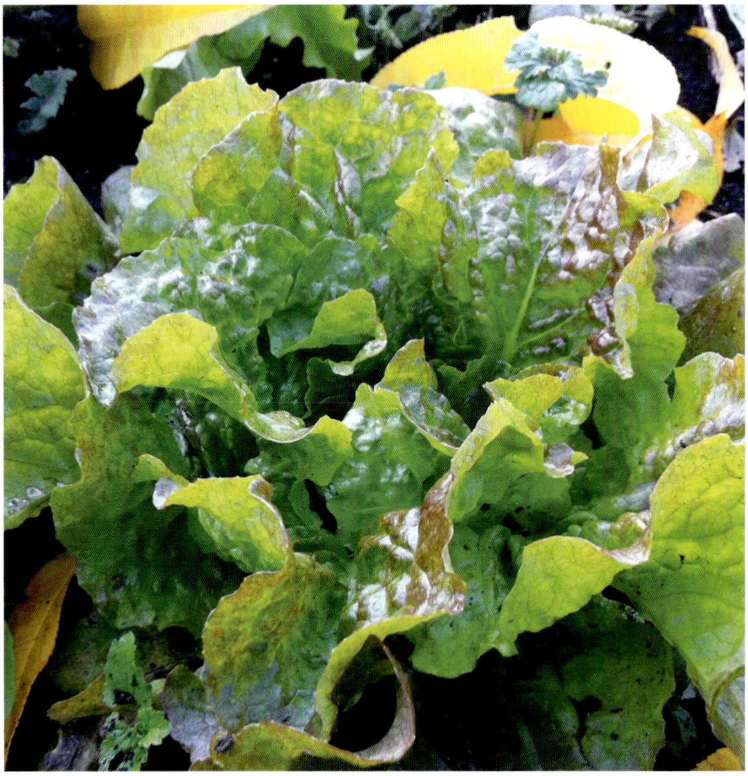

A School Lunch Revolution

Alice Waters

Penguin Press
New York
2025

PENGUIN PRESS
An imprint of Penguin Random House LLC
1745 Broadway, New York, NY 10019
penguinrandomhouse.com

Copyright © 2025 by Alice Waters

Penguin Random House values and supports copyright. Copyright fuels creativity, encourages diverse voices, promotes free speech and creates a vibrant culture. Thank you for buying an authorized edition of this book and for complying with copyright laws by not reproducing, scanning, or distributing any part of it in any form without permission. You are supporting writers and allowing Penguin Random House to continue to publish books for every reader. Please note that no part of this book may be used or reproduced in any manner for the purpose of training artificial intelligence technologies or systems.

Photographs courtesy of Don Hicks and Patricia Curtan.
Illustrations courtesy of Patricia Curtan.

Book design by Patricia Curtan

LIBRARY OF CONGRESS CATALOGING-IN-PUBLICATION DATA
Names: Waters, Alice, author.
Title: A school lunch revolution / Alice Waters.
Description: New York : Penguin Press, 2025.
Identifiers: LCCN 2024041612 (print) | LCCN 2024041613 (ebook) | ISBN 9780525561569 (hardcover) | ISBN 9780525561576 (ebook)
Subjects: LCSH: Chez Panisse | Seasonal cooking. | Luncheons. | LCGFT: Cookbooks.
Classification: LCC TX714 .W2785 2025 (print) | LCC TX714 (ebook) | DDC 641.5/3—dc23/eng/20241029
LC record available at https://lccn.loc.gov/2024041612
LC ebook record available at https://lccn.loc.gov/2024041613

Printed in China
1 3 5 7 9 10 8 6 4 2

The recipes contained in this book have been created for the ingredients and techniques indicated. The Publisher is not responsible for your specific health or allergy needs that may require supervision. Nor is the Publisher responsible for any adverse reactions you may have to the recipes contained in the book, whether you follow them as written or modify them to suit your personal dietary needs or tastes.

The authorized representative in the EU for product safety and compliance is Penguin Random House Ireland, Morrison Chambers, 32 Nassau Street, Dublin D02 YH68, Ireland, https://eu-contact.penguin.ie.

To all the gifted educators who have nurtured the
Edible Schoolyard for thirty years and inspired a network of
6,500 similar programs around the world

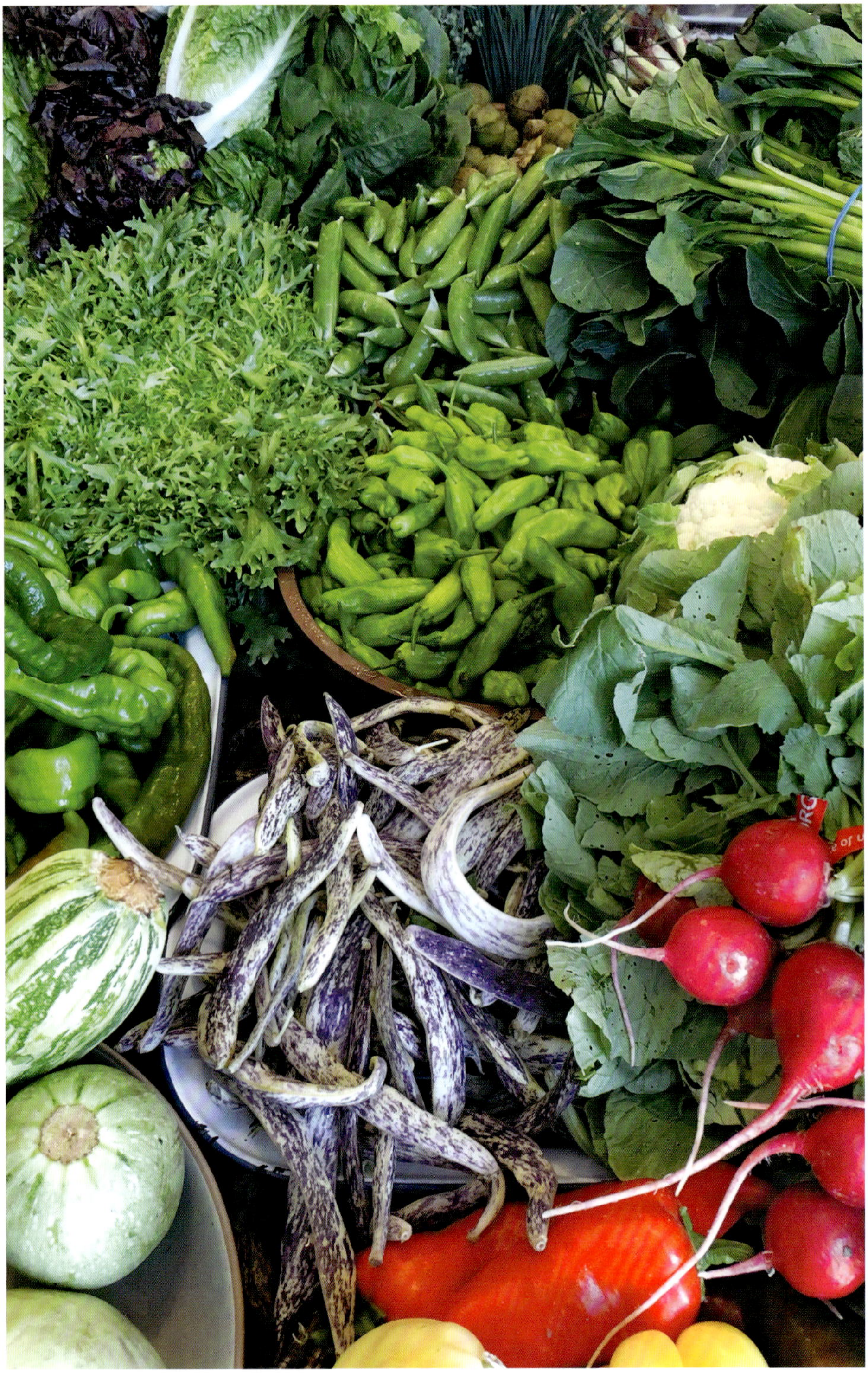

Contents

A School Lunch Revolution   1

Menu Staples   21

Salads   25

Sauces   35

Breads and Grains   45

Beans and Legumes   57

Noodles and Rice   65

Soups   77

Meats and Stews   91

Vegetables   105

Fruits   115

Breakfast   123

Pickles and Preserves   133

Seasonal Menus   145

Acknowledgments   152

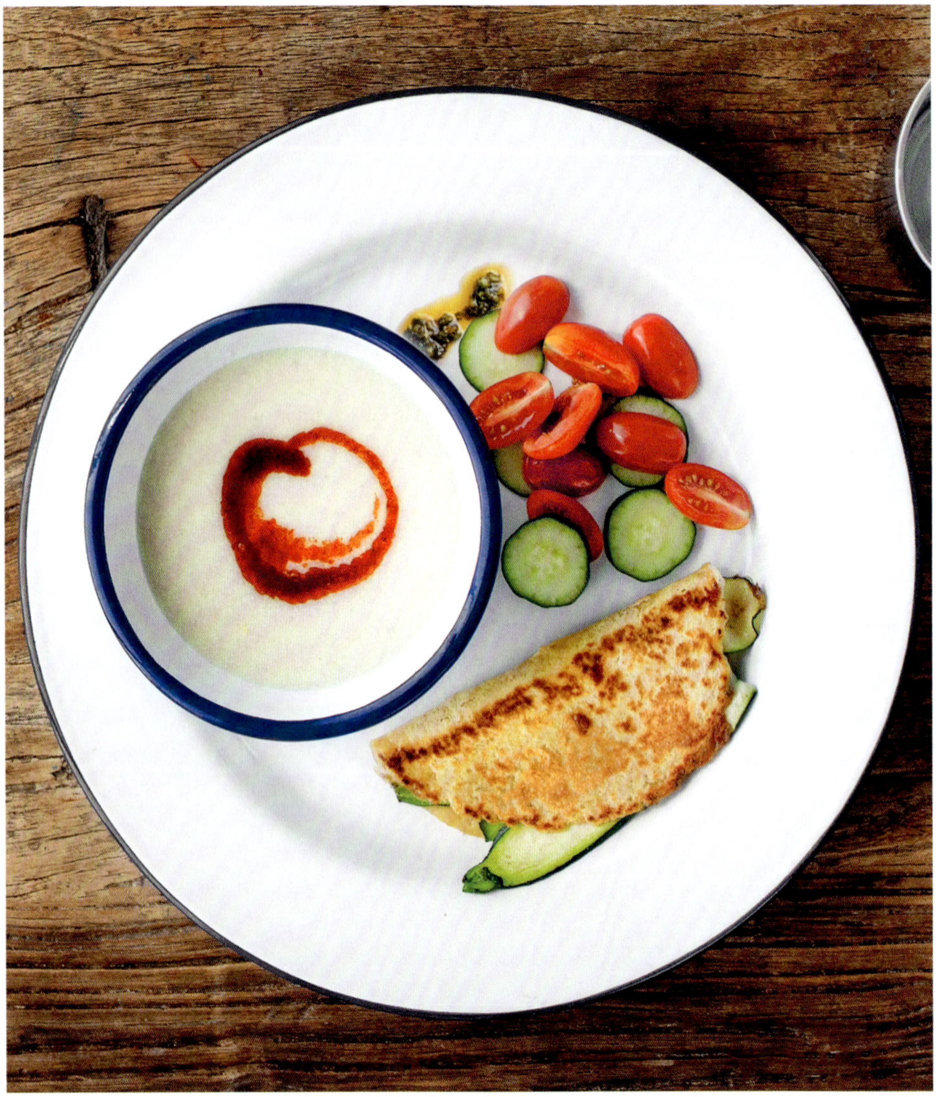

A School Lunch Revolution

Education and food are two universal rights. All children deserve to go to school. And everyone deserves to eat nourishing food. These two rights are at the foundation of our health and well-being. We are at a pivotal moment: if we truly want to address the intersecting systemic problems of health, education, and climate change, we must take action *now*. This is not the time for half measures—we are in a battle for the future of our planet. A significant action we can take right now is to reimagine our food systems and the way we feed our students, from kindergarten all the way through high school and college. What I am proposing is a direct, meaningful relationship between schools and farms: I call this school-supported regenerative agriculture. Unlike the existing system for school lunch, this holistic approach to feeding students includes buying ingredients from regenerative farmers and producers and cooking those fresh ingredients on-site in school kitchens. If schools purchased, cooked, and served food in this way—buying *directly* from organic, regenerative farmers—it would not merely transform the food in cafeterias and the health and happiness of our students (although of course it would). It could also transform our climate.

I travel a great deal and speak to all kinds of gatherings—to anyone who will listen!—about the imperative of feeding our schoolchildren healthy food, supporting farmers who practice regenerative agriculture, and looking at climate change through the lens of food and health. Talk is good, but occasionally I have the opportunity to try to convince people the best way I know how: with food. Taste this peach—this is what we could serve to our children.

I have seen how it works when, for example, we served a school lunch menu to six hundred organic farmers at an annual farming conference in Georgia. I wanted them to experience what I have seen firsthand. For the past twenty-five years, I have been thinking about and reimagining school food at the Edible Schoolyard Project, a kitchen and garden classroom at a public middle school in Berkeley, California. Over the years, we have developed recipes that are nourishing, delicious, affordable, and universally loved by students and adults alike.

All the ingredients for our lunch in Georgia were sourced locally within fifty miles, direct from the farmers, who were so proud to bring us their beautiful organic produce. Before lunch I spoke of our goals and vision and asked that everyone imagine themselves in a school setting, sitting with a group of twelve, and each with a task of serving the others. The farmers began to chat while we filled a long serving table with platters of reezy peezy fritters and cornbread, bowls of collard greens, roasted root vegetables, and green salad. When all was ready, to avoid the chaos and din of typical cafeterias, I asked the group to quietly bring the food to the dining tables. In three and a half minutes the room of six hundred was served peacefully, calmly, and without rush. They passed the bowls and platters at the table and began to take in the aromas, colors, and warmth, and the conversation welled up—all about the food! *This tastes really delicious, it's so simple, why is it so good?* And that is when it hit home for the farmers: *This* is what school lunch can be, when it is made from local, seasonal ingredients. Imagine the possibilities if we fed our children this way.

When school districts buy food from local regenerative farms, they contribute to the economic empowerment of our communities, revitalizing and supporting farms that are taking care of the land for future generations. But just as important, they perpetuate the essential values of stewardship, nourishment, and interconnectedness directly through the cafeteria doors to our students.

The recipes and menus in this book are examples of what is possible when school-supported regenerative agriculture is at the foundation of a school lunch revolution. Throughout, the recipes are guided by the principles of what school lunch should be: Local and Seasonal, Affordable, Diverse, Simple and Delicious, and Beautiful.

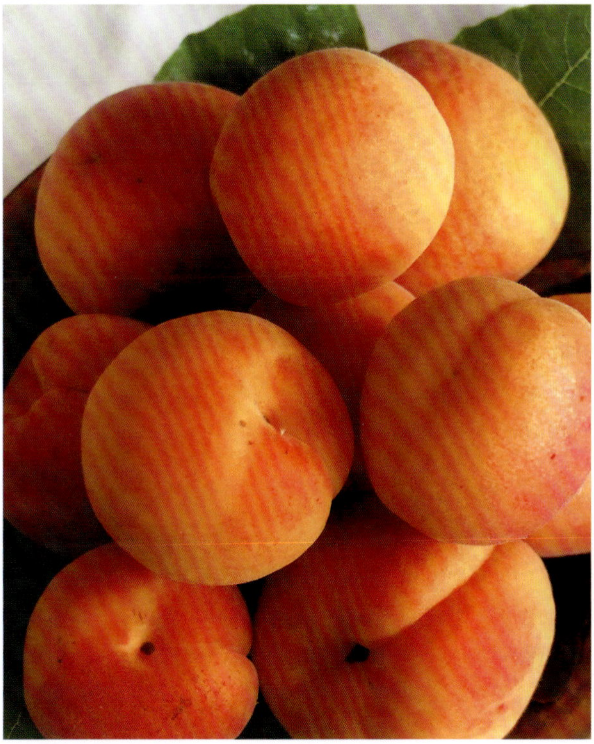

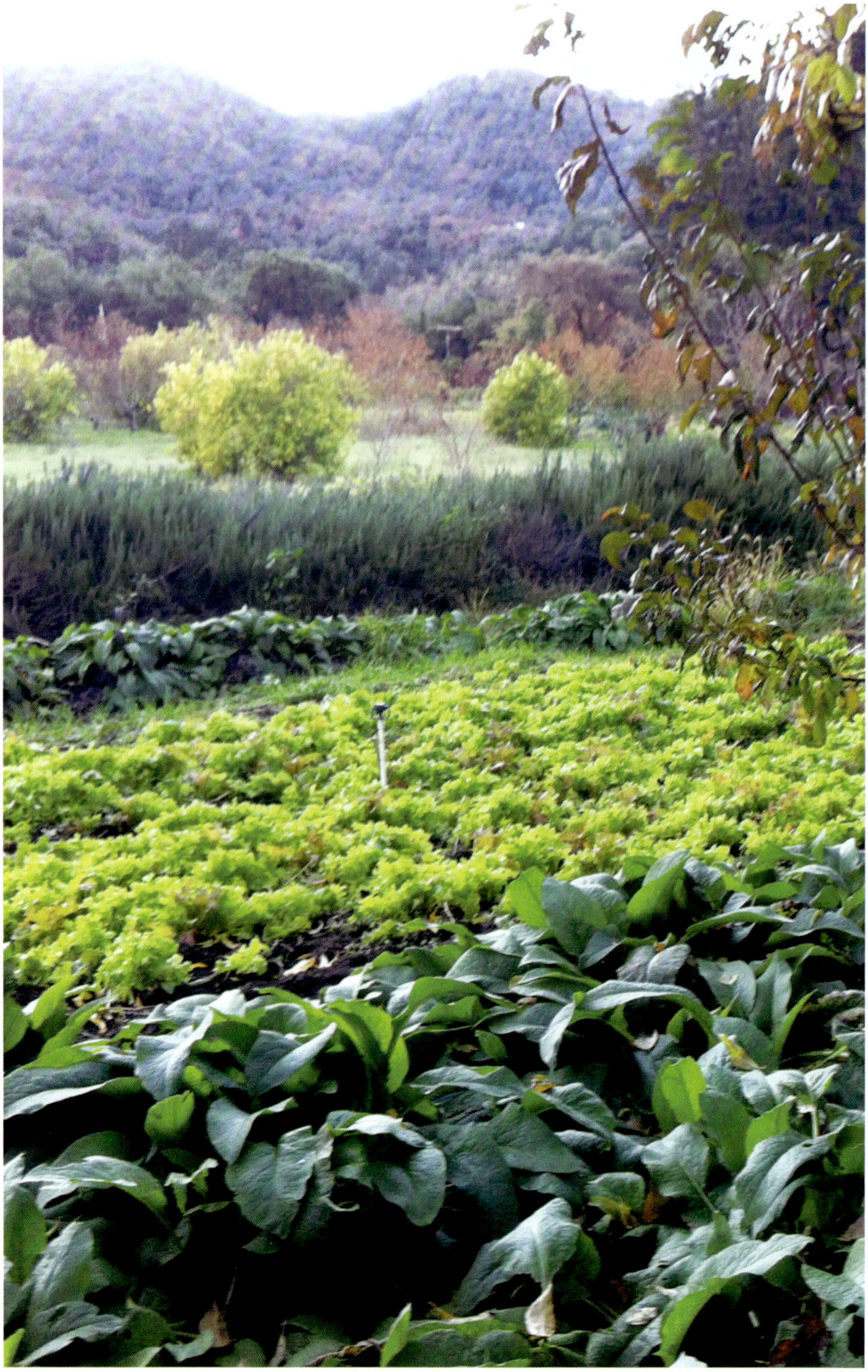

School-Supported Regenerative Organic Agriculture

School-supported agriculture would work much like community-supported agriculture programs, or CSAs. In a CSA, consumers and growers pledge mutual support to one another; consumers agree to pay for whatever farmers are growing, and every week, farmers provide them with the best of what is in season at that moment. CSAs give farmers financial security that isn't contingent on the success or failure of any one crop or harvest throughout the year; at the same time, CSAs help educate their communities about season and place by creating a vital, direct bond between consumers and their local farmers. That is why the concept is school lunch *plus* regenerative agriculture. They support each other and the link is vital for the economies of both. I cannot conceive of one without the other.

For decades, Chez Panisse has been buying food directly from the farmers, ranchers, and fishers who protect the land and treat their employees with care and dignity. Crucially, buying food in this way didn't cost the restaurant any more than it would if we were buying food in the "conventional" way through distributors. Without a distributor middleman taking a cut, we have been able to pay farmers the real cost of their food so they could pay their farm workers fairly and take care of their land. The restaurant provided the farmers and ranchers with purchasing security, and in return something magical and unintended happened over the years: the farmers started to educate us. They taught us that the food that's in season is the most delicious. They taught us about local biodiversity. They taught us that our health, and the health of the planet, is in the soil.

Schools are some of our largest purchasers of food in the United States, and school-supported agriculture would be an instant economic stimulus for regenerative farms. Regenerative agriculture is beyond just organic, which rejects the use of harmful chemicals. It is the practice of farming that rebuilds, restores, and supports the organic matter that composes healthy soil. *Organic* and *regenerative* are terms that overlap with each other, but I like to use both, as they are equally important and necessary indicators of a farm's agricultural practices. While regenerative farming is not yet regulated by the USDA, organic farming is, and in some states, such as California and Oregon, the standards for organic certification are even higher than the USDA's standards.

We now know that everything the organic regenerative farmers and ranchers have done to take care of their land and their animals has also been actively removing carbon from the atmosphere and putting it in the ground where it belongs. There has been a direct, achievable solution to climate change all along—and it is right under our feet. Regenerative organic farming restores and even *improves* our soil's natural ability to hold and sequester carbon, because it treats the soil underground as the rich and diverse living ecosystem that it can be. This feels like revolutionary agricultural technology, but it is the way that farmers have taken care of the land for millennia; this traditional knowledge has now been scientifically tested and is ready for immediate and wide-scale implementation.

But it is not just about helping balance the climate. More carbon in the soil increases the soil's water-holding capacity, which makes the soil more resilient in the face of droughts and flooding. Just a 1 percent increase in the soil's organic matter means a single acre can hold twenty thousand more gallons of water. We can use the excess carbon in the atmosphere to rebuild functioning and healthy living soil—and that healthy soil could be what saves us.

While the platonic ideal of school-supported agriculture is a farmer bringing produce right to the door of the cafeteria, this model might need adjusting in some cases, given the scale and volume of school food procurement. What's vital is that we connect schools more closely with farmers and food producers. Instead of an extractive, for-profit middleman, which is the predominant model right now, some school districts may benefit from a nonprofit food hub, farm cooperative, or public-private partnership that subsidizes the work of collecting and distributing food. A reimagined food hub could serve many purposes, from compost facilitator to food service culinary training center to a gathering place for farmers, chefs, families, volunteers, and the community.

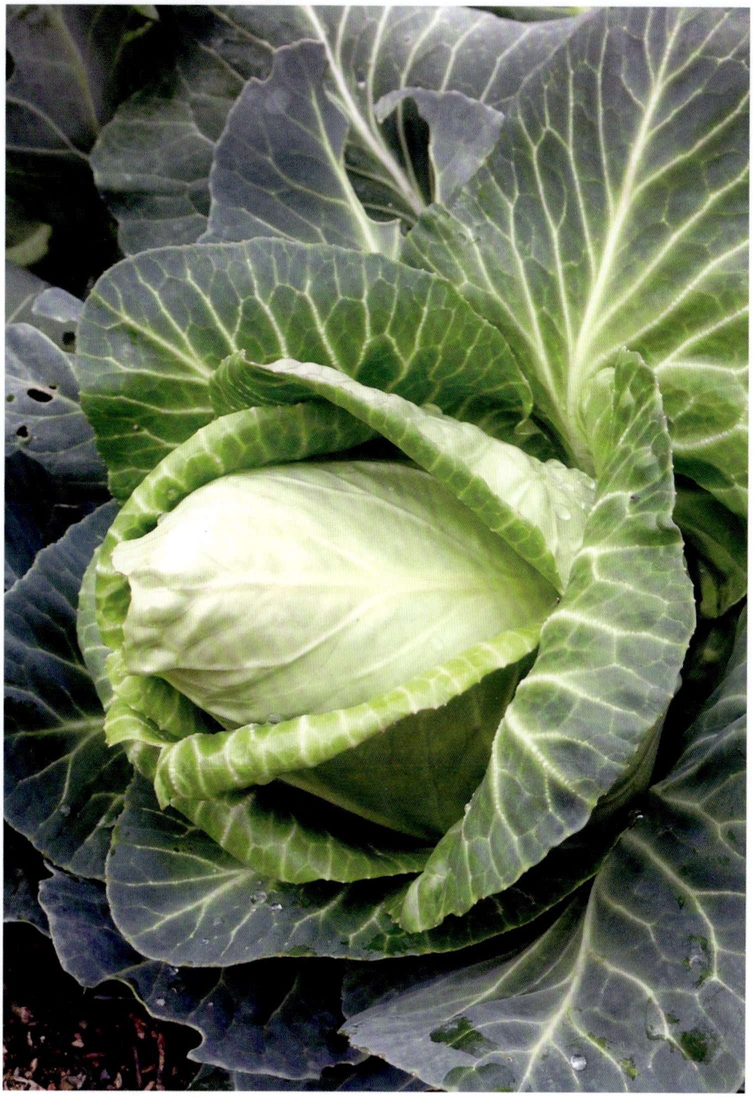

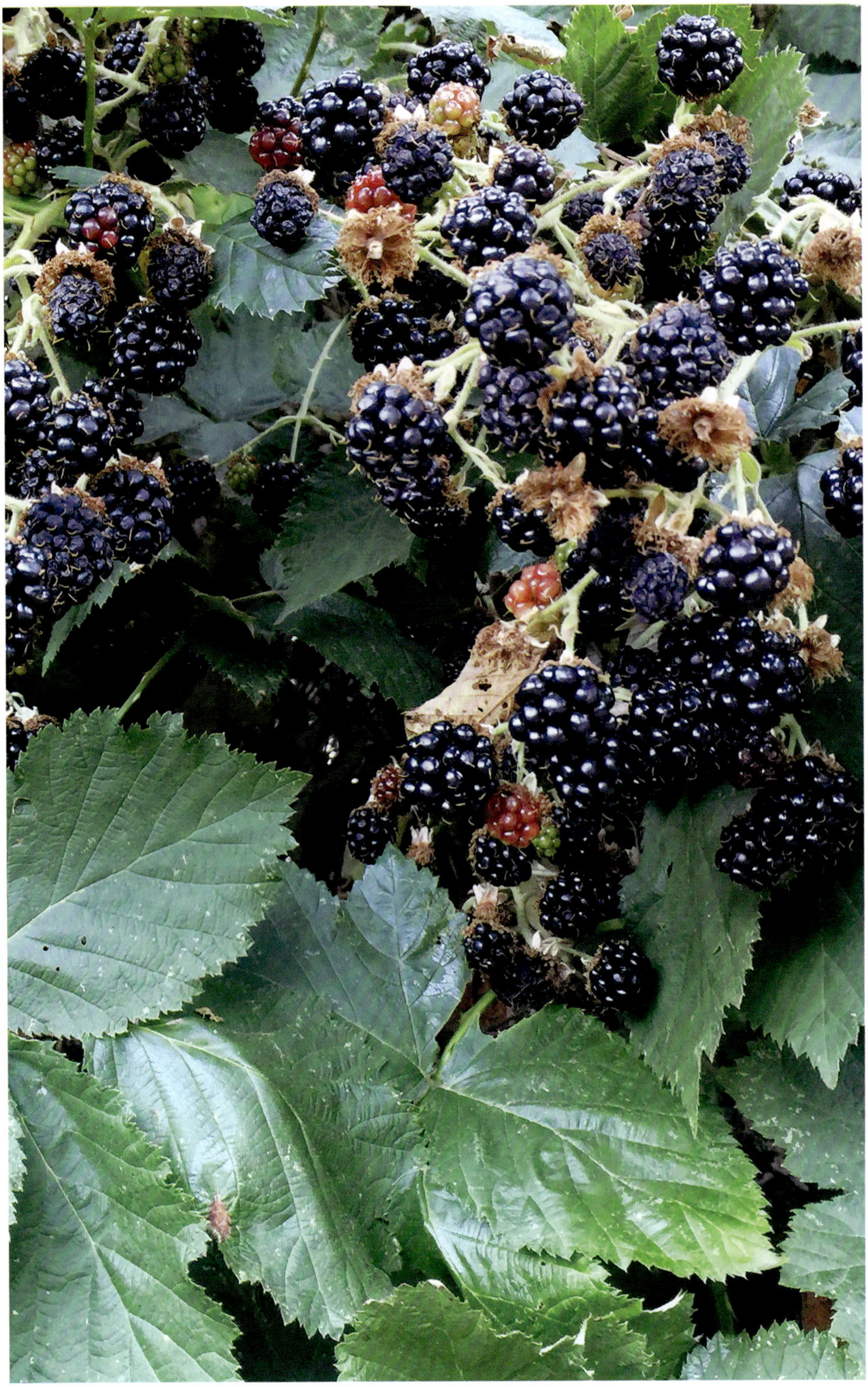

Local and Seasonal

I have been running Chez Panisse for fifty-four years now. I started the restaurant in 1971 after living in France for a year and training in London to be a Montessori teacher. I was looking for the kind of flavor and beauty of food I had experienced in France in the 1960s. The fruits and vegetables I had seen in the French markets were fresh, alive, vibrant, delicious—and that was what I wanted everyone to experience when they came to Chez Panisse. My pursuit of taste brought me to the doorsteps of local organic farmers and producers. These small California farmers operated entirely differently than the industrial farms in the United States, which prioritized transportability and profits over flavor and health. The organic farmers grew flavorful heirloom varieties of vegetables, or raised heritage breeds; they harvested their crops at peak ripeness. And you could taste the difference.

The most important decision we made at Chez Panisse was to buy only local and seasonal foods. When we did that, it created new inspiration and challenges for the chefs; it opened up a world of winter vegetables we'd never considered. Suddenly we were making celery root soup in the winter, seeing a whole rainbow of carrots we never knew existed. It made us wait in anticipation for the ripe tomatoes in July. And when they were over, they were over, and we moved on to the next harvest. Eating in season is a deep and inspiring worldview that connects you to nature, to the bounty of the land around you, to the rhythm of your own life. And it is exciting for students, too—they aren't participating in the tedious, flavorless routine of eating the same second-rate, out-of-season fruits and vegetables all year long. When you cook seasonally, you experience the inspiration that comes from constantly changing ingredients, not from unlimited availability. Students learn to look forward to the moment when strawberries are at their sweetest, or the time in late spring when snap peas finally arrive at the table.

This is the true definition of farm to table, a procurement model that puts the farmer first: we commit to buying whatever our producers tell us is ripe and ready and delicious at that moment—and make our meals accordingly. Of course, this means we have to cook differently throughout the year, and there are times of the year when certain foods aren't available.

As recently as 1950, Americans mostly ate food that was in season and locally produced, except for maybe imported coffee, tea, and spices. I grew up in New Jersey, where the families I knew would can and preserve fruits and vegetables for the winter, store food, and use greenhouses to grow food through harsher seasons. Cooking in this way is not only what is right for the planet, it is deeply pleasurable—because you cannot have truly delicious food unless it is picked when it's ripe and eaten soon after.

I can say all of this with conviction because I have seen that it is possible to create a program that rethinks food, seasonality, and education from the ground up. In the Edible Schoolyard Project garden and kitchen classrooms, we use a hands-on approach to teach academic subjects to a thousand teenage students, a population of children who speak twenty-two different languages at home. That one school has inspired a network of more than 6,200 like-minded programs around the world.

I have watched the transformations in these programs. I have seen how students are empowered when they learn about the world through food, and how it changes their relationship to the environment and the food they eat. At the Edible Schoolyard Project, we are teaching middle school students, young teenagers at a tricky transitional time; you might not think of them as the most persuadable audience. And yet they fall in love with real food when they are the ones planting it, growing it themselves, watching it ripen, learning when to harvest and how to cook it. We always like to say that it's only six weeks to kale: that's how long it takes for students new to the program to start eating—and loving!—kale.

But more than simply learning to love fruits and vegetables, students are learning about their place in the natural world. When schools are working in partnership with regenerative farmers and producers, serving food to students that is ripe and delicious, it activates students in the way they yearn for—giving them an instant connection to the seasons, an understanding of our ever-changing climate, and a respect for the land and the people who grew their food.

Affordable

"Organic school lunch sounds great, but it's just too expensive." This is the statement I hear the most often from skeptics—and even from some believers. And it's a large part of why my colleagues and I started this book by challenging ourselves to make menus and cook dishes that fell within the guidelines of the USDA's school lunch reimbursement program. (At the time of this writing, the 2023–2024 reimbursable rate for each student's lunch is $4.25; for breakfast, the reimbursement rate is $2.28.) We set other guidelines for ourselves as well: use only seasonal, local, organic produce (bought at retail prices, not wholesale); prioritize grains, beans, vegetables, and fruits; and minimize portion sizes of meats and poultry. What we found was that it *is* possible to create nutritious lunches from organic food, all at a surprisingly affordable price. When you are buying locally and seasonally, food is inherently more affordable; you aren't paying the premium it costs to have cherry tomatoes shipped in from abroad in the dead of winter. You are taking advantage of the low cost of ingredients when they're abundant, and then using those foods strategically.

The Italian term *cucina povera* refers to the centuries-old concept of making delicious and nurturing food with simple, inexpensive ingredients. These sorts of ingredients are far removed from the modern fast-food idea of cheap, ultra-processed foods; when I think of cucina povera, for example, I think of a bowl of warm cannellini beans with fruity olive oil and crusty bread. Of course, the same concept is found in every society, and it is the traditional way people have always fed themselves. It is the very opposite of processed or prepackaged food. The irony is that processed foods are not only less healthy and less satisfying, but more expensive.

Affordability is about not just the cost of ingredients but also the cost and demands of time and labor needed to prepare fresh food. There are a growing number of inspiring programs and organizations across the country staffed with talented, experienced professionals—many of them former restaurant chefs—doing fantastic work with school districts to train and transition local teams to cooking on-site with fresh ingredients. This dedicated and practical work demonstrates that change is possible and achievable—and it dignifies the entire process of working in school kitchens, empowering cooks to think creatively about the foods and methods available to them.

Diverse

The recipes in this book take their inspiration from a diversity of food traditions, from Mexico to China to Morocco to Thailand. We want everyone to have an appreciation for foods from around the world and the ways that different cultures have been nourishing people for centuries. Every culture makes nutritious, affordable, delicious food. It is at the core of who we are as diverse societies. When we make those cross-cultural connections based on food and share ideas and cuisines, it brings students into a new relationship with other traditions as well. It is like having a cultural ambassador from another country visit you at the table: food is an accessible, immediate, sensory connection to other cultures, other ways of life.

Diverse local foods are available across the country, whether you live in Arizona or in Maine. Every area has seasonal crops that are distinct in that region. It is possible to find fresh vegetables in winter as well as other seasons, thanks to greenhouses and adaptive practices—and in the months when fresh vegetables are harder to come by, we can make creative use of what is stocked in our pantries: whole grains and flours, dried beans, dried fruits, preserves, spices, pickles, nuts, fermented foods, seeds, and oils.

Variety and diversity of flavor can be easily accomplished with even a basic array of spices and seasonings. In the kitchen classroom at the Edible Schoolyard Project, we keep a spice cabinet available to students, who can take whatever they would like to add to the dish they're cooking—cumin, coriander, paprika, chiles, herbs, and peppers. And it's amazing how excited they are to flavor their own foods. The American fast-food diet, saturated in sugar and salt, has deadened our palates—but there is a whole universe of flavor at our fingertips.

Diversity is also about the breathtaking biodiversity that exists when we push beyond the limited agricultural range of industrial farms. Since the rise of industrial agriculture, the number of fruit and vegetable varieties has dwindled to almost nothing; the only varieties that survive in the industrial agricultural model are the ones selected to withstand weeks of shipping and storage. We need to support and embrace the incredible biodiversity that was commonplace on our farms only seventy years ago, and that still exists on regenerative farms today: there are thousands of types of apples beyond the ever-present Red Delicious, for example, each with its own distinct taste. This vast, beautiful array of flavor, color, texture, and form exists for almost any food you can think of—lettuces, tomatoes, melons, beans, potatoes, mushrooms—and has the power to surprise and delight children and adults alike. Biodiversity is what makes food so exciting—but it also has a much more profound environmental importance. The more we can support and encourage crop biodiversity, the better our chances of surviving crop failures and withstanding the increasing pressures of a rapidly warming planet on our food supply.

Simple and Delicious

If the food we're serving isn't delicious, children aren't going to eat it. It is that simple. But *delicious* does not mean fatty, starchy, sugary foods, as the fast-food industry would love for you to think, and *simple* does not mean bland or unadventurous. School lunch has long been relegated to the category of "kid food," which is largely disconnected from the way we eat in the rest of our lives—but I believe children are much more discerning than we give them credit for. The idea of the picky eater has loomed so large for so long—and indeed, the fast-food industry loves to reinforce this idea to maximize their profits—that it's easy to forget that children are naturally curious. They love to learn about and taste the food traditions from cultures around the globe. The recipes in this book are designed to engage children's senses: there are foods for dipping and eating with your hands, flavorful sauces, a play of colors and textures that inspire students to explore and learn.

One approach to simplicity is to simplify the menu. I believe in offering students one well-balanced, seasonal menu a day; the menu should change daily and have allowances for food allergies or sensitivities, but it is one menu that everyone eats. When there are too many options available, it allows students to stay in food ruts, make the so-called safe choices that they have made many times before. A simplified menu also encourages cooks to focus their labor on the organization of the single meal, which means they can make the food more carefully and thoughtfully. And when everyone is having the shared experience of eating the same meal together, it is community-building in a subtle but significant way.

And the great secret is this: when food is ripe and delicious, you don't have to do very much to it. At the Edible Schoolyard Project, we have found that students respond when foods are more identifiable as the whole foods themselves: instead of eating a chopped-up romaine salad, for example, at times they're getting whole romaine leaves, whole radishes, and a vinaigrette to dip them in as they choose. Food that is ripe and in season can remain simple, recognizable—and it reinforces children's connection to the plant itself, and to nature.

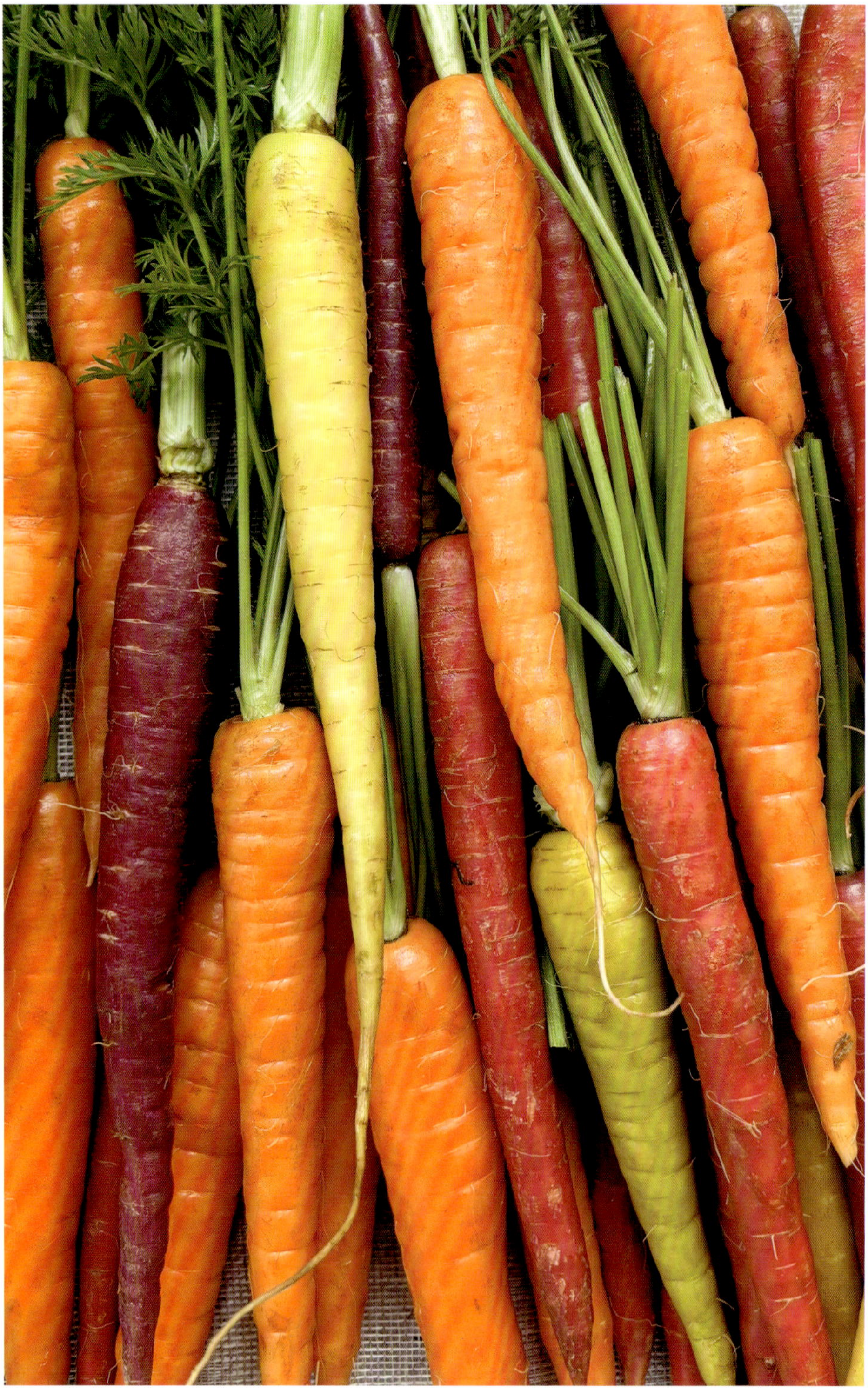

BEAUTIFUL

What does beauty mean in a school food context? One of the foundational beliefs of the Edible Schoolyard Project is that beauty is a language of care. This means that when students encounter something that has been beautifully prepared for them, they understand, intuitively, that they are cared for and valued. We want to nourish bodies, but we want to nourish more than that. We want to nourish students' spirits and their sense of community.

School cafeterias are often thought of as particularly unlovely spaces: crowded, institutional, and exceptionally resistant to beautification efforts. And while this can be true in some cases, I have also seen how spaces can be creatively transformed. A local school without a cafeteria converts a gymnasium every day into an inviting space where students can sit down and eat together, with tables thoughtfully set with flowers and bowls of fruit, and pictures and posters of food and farms on the walls. A typical school in Japan has the students rearrange their desks into two communal tables when it is time to eat, and small carts deliver lunch to their classrooms. In very large schools with limited cafeteria spaces, it is possible to schedule staggered lunchtimes so that students are able to enjoy a more personalized, calm experience.

These strategies are not just for aesthetic purposes—they exist so that everyone feels safe, accepted, and invited to participate. I have always imagined school kitchens and cafeterias as places that should be designed to welcome volunteers. Places where parents, relatives, elders, and community members can come together to shell peas, peel garlic, or help with other simple food-preparation tasks, and even join the students at the table for meals. Spaces with natural light where the preparation, produce, and food are visible and on display, and the hardworking staff are seen, respected, and appreciated. I have visited high schools that have dedicated culinary arts programs where students help prepare the food for their community.

Students of all ages yearn to be taken seriously in this way, to be trusted with meaningful work—and students take pride in learning real skills and doing the essential work of making meals for others.

The lunch experience is a powerful educational opportunity. Students can learn about nutrition and where their food comes from and develop lasting healthy eating habits. Zero-waste practices are models of climate action: using attractive washable dishes, utensils, cups, and glasses; sorting organic matter to return to the farms for compost; eliminating plastics and throwaways.

I would love to see more time given to the midday lunch break. Time to eat at a relaxed pace, and time for students to participate in the process of serving, clearing, and caring for their shared spaces. Time to get to know the kitchen staff and to help out, and time even to prepare and cook their own food as they do in the Edible Schoolyard kitchen classroom. I envision treating the lunch hour as more of an intentional learning experience. Students have asked me before, "Why isn't the food in the cafeteria like the food we have here in the Edible Schoolyard classroom?" It is an important question. Lunchtime is a moment to eat, yes, but it is also a moment for students to be active and engaged creators of their own environment and experience. Their participation is what gives them an appreciation for the food on their plates, for the traditions, foodways, farmers, and cooks that contributed to its deliciousness, and for the beauty and potential of the natural world around them.

When students are sitting around the table, eating and talking together, they are also learning about the fundamental values of civility and democracy. They are understanding how to work together with respect and dignity. They are learning the language of care.

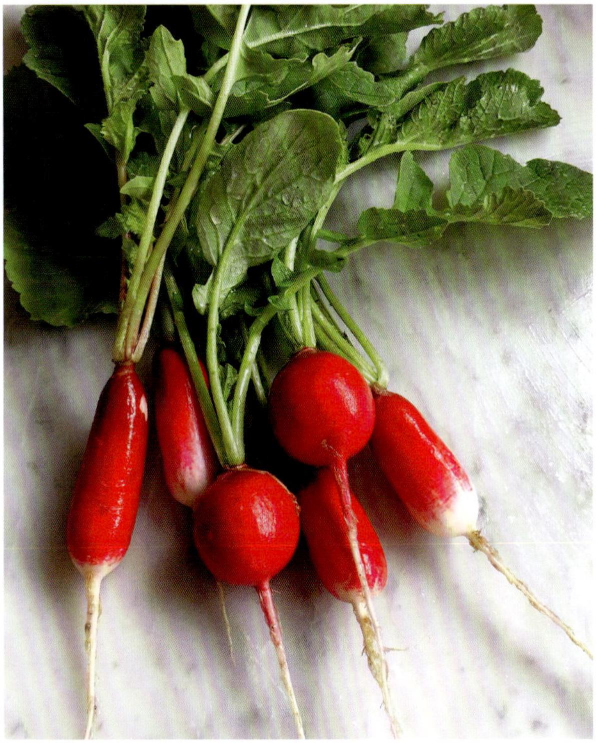

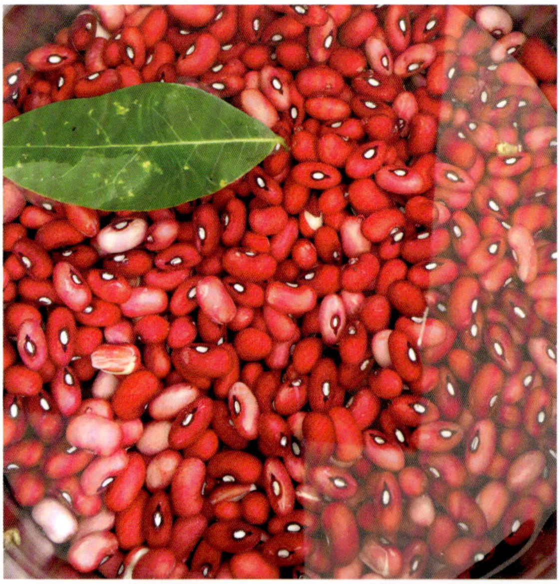
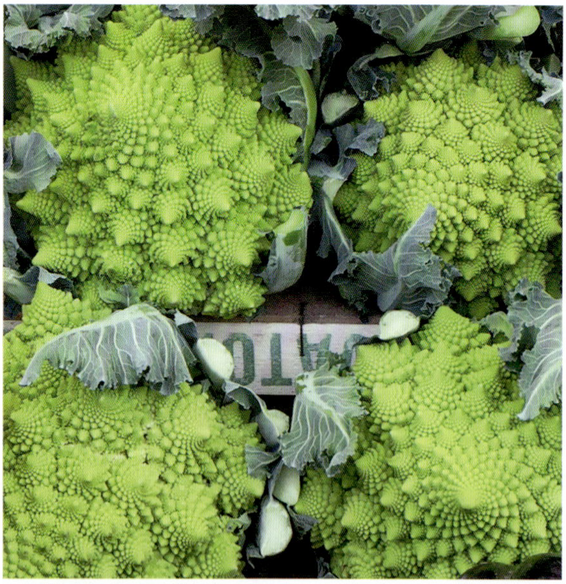
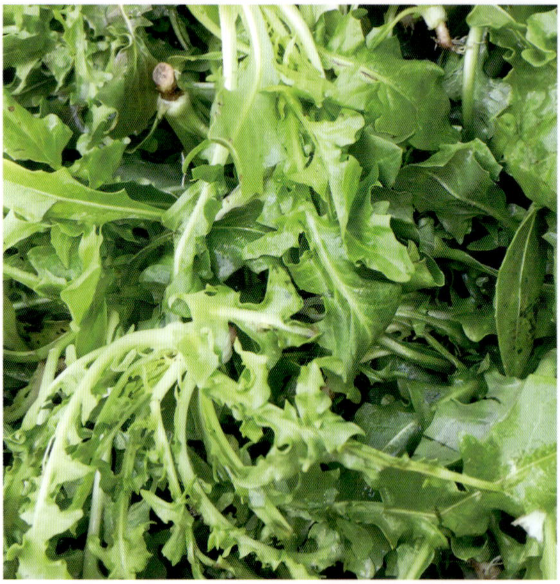
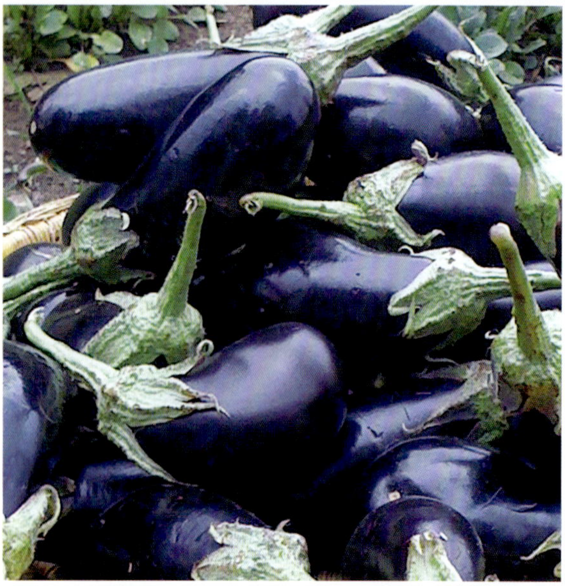
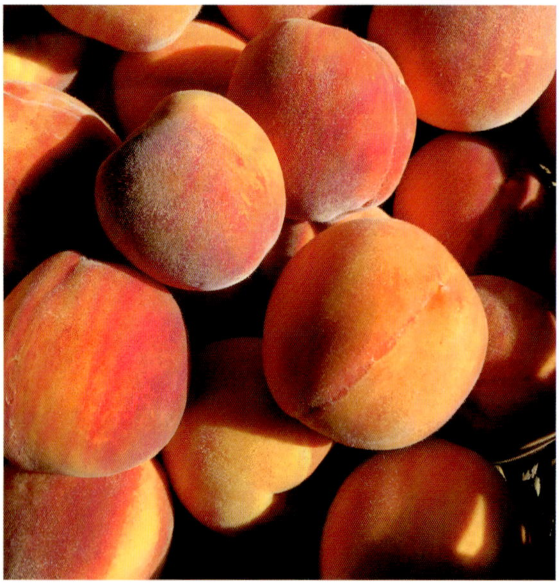
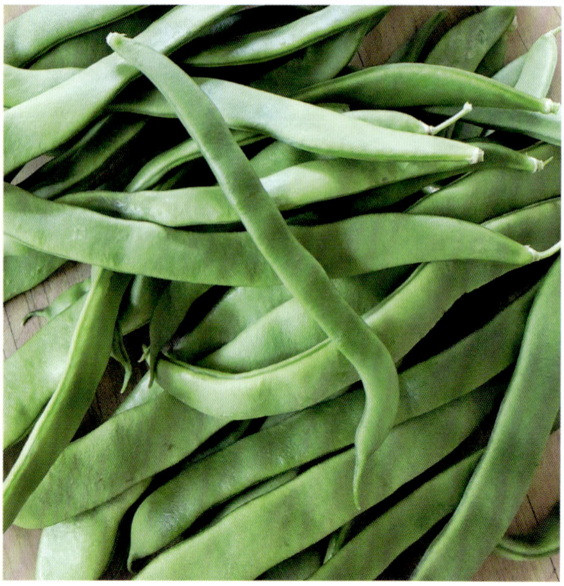

Menu Staples

A practical approach to creating and planning menus is to develop a repertoire of staple dishes—building blocks—that are economical in time and cost, seasonally and culturally flexible, and delicious.

These staple recipes are organized in general categories to facilitate menu planning. The recipes are representative examples of methods and techniques that can be varied with different seasonal ingredients and flavorings, scaled up to large quantities, and combined and rearranged to make versatile satisfying menus. With repetition and practice, the cooking becomes comfortable, known, and reliable.

Seasonality, when produce is at its best and most abundant, can provide an easy and inspirational starting point: beautiful leeks and potatoes for a soup or gratin; zucchini and tomatoes for a pesto pasta; sweet potatoes to oven roast; spinach and kale greens to sauté with garlic; sweet carrots for a bright shaved vegetable salad. Start with one dish, pair it with another selection from the repertoire, and the menu begins to take shape.

A NOTE ABOUT SALT

The recipes call for kosher salt, which is different from table salt. Kosher salt is lighter than table salt because of its large grain size. The flakes are airy and coarse, which makes it easy to pick up and sprinkle over food. It is a mined salt and not iodized and so has a clean and pure flavor with no aftertaste. Because it is less dense than fine table salt, it should not be used in a one-to-one ratio. If substituting one type for the other, use a ratio of 1¼ teaspoons kosher salt to 1 teaspoon table salt. Sea salt is made from evaporated seawater. Different sources and methods yield flakes of various sizes and density that contain trace minerals and flavors. Whatever type of salt is used, taste is always the ultimate guide. Taste as you go when seasoning to find the right balance and get the most flavor out of what you are cooking.

Salads 25
   Green Salad
   Tomato Salad
   Caesar Salad
   Apple and Cabbage Slaw
   Napa Cabbage Slaw
   Shaved Carrot Salad
   Miso-Sesame Cucumbers
   Tabbouleh

Sauces 35
   Vinaigrette
   Aioli
   Raita
   Salsa Verde
   Tomato Sauce

Breads and Grains 45
   Cornbread
   Polenta
   Flatbread
   Pita Bread
   Millet Muffins
   Focaccia
   Edible Schoolyard Loaf

Beans and Legumes 57
   Cranberry Beans
   Black-Eyed Peas
   Falafel
   Yellow Lentil Dal
   Hummus

Noodles and Rice 65
   Pesto Pasta and Tomatoes
   Basil and Sunflower Seed Pesto
   Chicken Noodle Soup
   Rice Noodle Salad
   Couscous
   Fried Rice
   Brown Rice
   Carrot and Cucumber Sushi
   Chicken Congee

Soups 77
   Butternut Squash Soup
   Corn Soup
   Minestrone
   Cannellini Beans
   Kale Pesto
   Garlic Toasts
   Cranberry Bean and Pasta Soup
   Leek and Potato Soup
   Green Lentil Soup
   Pozole

Meats and Stews 91
    Barbecue Chicken Legs
    Barbecue Sauce
    Meatballs and Tomato Sauce
    Spicy Lamb Meatballs
    Spicy Meatball Sauce
    Chile Braised Pork Tacos
    Tomato Salsa
    Chicken Tomato Curry
    Chickpeas and Brown Rice
    Red Bean Chili
    Red Beans

Vegetables 105
    Sautéed Corn with Chile and Lime
    Baby Bok Choy and Tamari Sauce
    Sweet Potato Wedges
    Mashed Potatoes and Celery Root
    Roasted Delicata Squash
    Sautéed Greens
    Collard Greens

Fruits 115
    Strawberry and Orange Bowl
    Summer Berry Compote
    Fall Fruit Cup
    Applesauce
    Baked Apples
    Baked Peaches
    Fruit Crumble

Breakfast 123
    Multigrain Porridge
    Oatmeal
    Granola
    Buttermilk Pancakes
    French Toast
    Quesadillas
    Potato Frittata
    Hard-Cooked Eggs

Pickles and Preserves 133
    Quick Pickles
    Pickled Red Cabbage
    Dill Pickles
    Fermented Pickles
    Kimchi
    Canned Tomatoes
    Tomato Confit
    Dried Fruits
    Frozen Berries

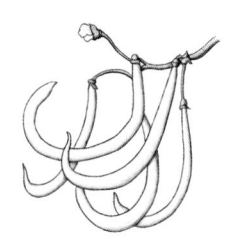

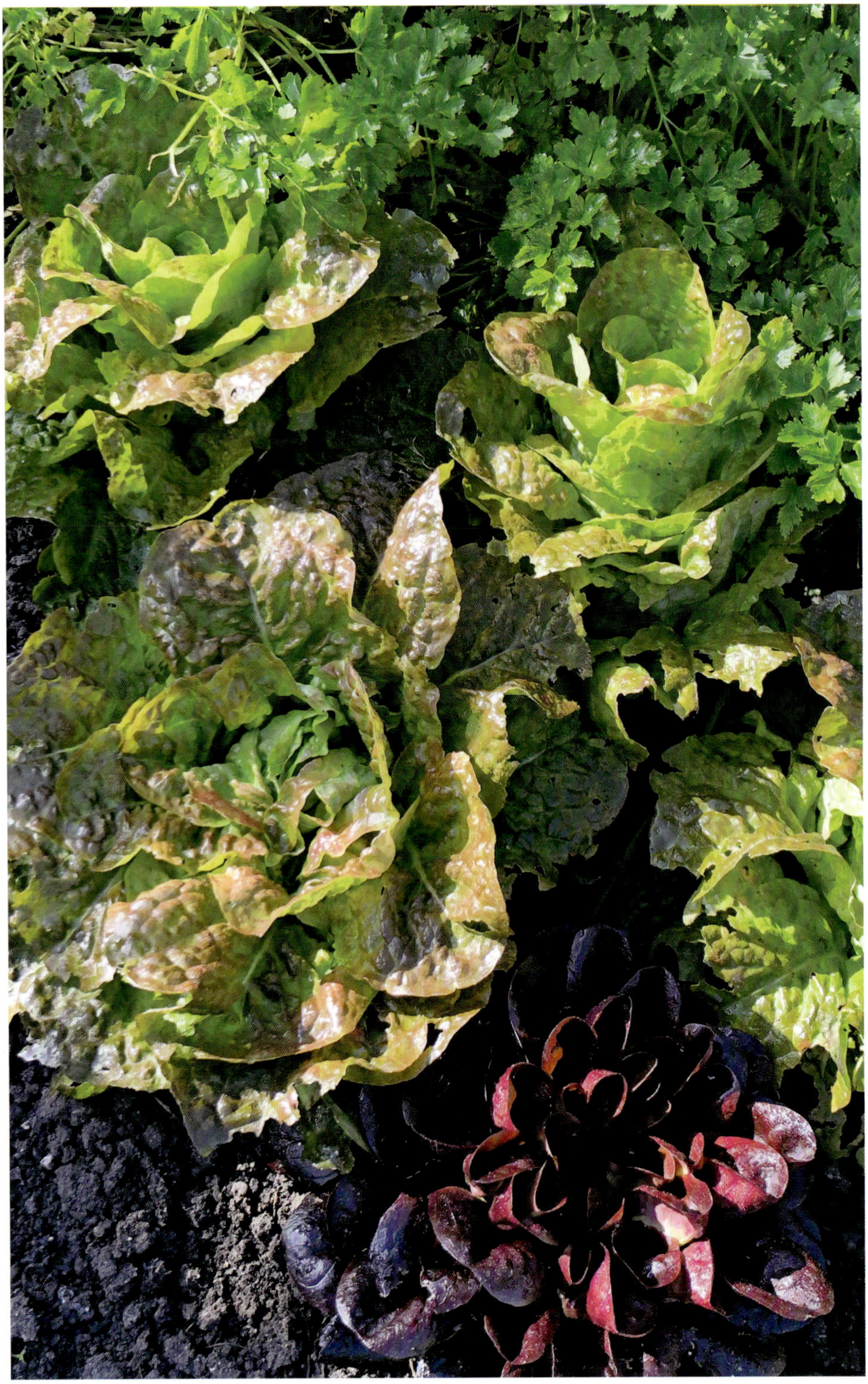

SALADS

Salad is an integral part of a lunch plate, but there is no one way to make it. A loose interpretation of salad welcomes all kinds of seasonal vegetables and fruits in many combinations—and not necessarily tossed or dressed in the usual way, but perhaps cut beautifully and served with a ramekin of vinaigrette, raita, or aioli for dipping to taste. Children love to make their own selections of what they like and how they choose to eat it.

A bright salad with lively flavors, colors, and textures provides a balancing contrast to cooked meats and grains and other substantial dishes. Salads bring the changing seasons onto the plate—tender lettuces, crunchy cabbage and romaine leaves, sweet carrots and fennel, juicy radishes and cucumbers, cherry tomatoes and big slicing tomatoes, beans of all kinds, fragrant herbs. Freshness is key.

Green Salad

For me, a salad is never a taken-for-granted side dish. A salad of fresh greens tossed with tart vinaigrette is a flavorful counterpoint that makes everything else on the plate taste better.

The seasons dictate the choice of lettuces and greens. Crisp and juicy romaine leaves, and the smaller Little Gem variety, are reliably available and perfect for zesty Caesar dressing or for dipping in vinaigrette and other sauces. I love a mixture of tender lettuces such as red and green oak leaf and butterhead lettuces, spicy red mustard, rocket (easy to grow in school gardens!), and tender herbs. Fall and winter salads of sturdy escarole, chicories, and lacy frisée make delicious salads, especially with the addition of fruits such as pears, apples, and persimmons, and toasted nuts.

MAKES 8 SERVINGS

4 heads romaine lettuce, or
  6 to 8 heads Little Gem lettuce, or
  2 or 3 heads tender lettuce
1 cup Vinaigrette (page 38)

To prepare the salad greens, trim the lettuce heads and separate the leaves. Gently wash the leaves in a basin of cold water, lift the lettuce out of the water, and place into a colander. If the lettuces are still dirty or sandy, wash again. Spin-dry the lettuces in batches in a salad spinner. Repeat if needed to make sure the lettuces are dry so that the dressing will not be diluted by water clinging to the leaves. Spread the leaves out on a towel in a single layer and roll up the towel, or layer the lettuces in a tub or container with towels between the layers, and refrigerate.

When ready to serve, if you like, tear or cut large leaves into smaller pieces. Put the lettuce in a spacious bowl and begin to add the dressing and toss gently. Use just enough dressing to coat the leaves lightly and evenly. Taste as you go and add more dressing as needed until the leaves are glistening but not overdressed and soggy. Finish with a sprinkling of salt and a squeeze of lemon or a splash of vinegar, if needed, to balance the salt and acid.

Tomato Salad

July, August, and September are when tomatoes are at their best and most flavorful. A salad of mixed tomatoes of different colors, varieties, and sizes is particularly beautiful. I always want a slice of crusty garlic toast with it to soak up the juices.

MAKES 8 SERVINGS

2 pounds ripe tomatoes (cherry tomatoes, heirloom, Early Girl)
2 small shallots
2 tablespoons red wine vinegar
Kosher salt and fresh-ground black pepper
½ cup olive oil
12 fresh basil leaves

For cherry tomatoes, stem, cut in half, and set aside in a bowl. Depending on their size, cut other tomatoes in wedges or slices.

Dice the shallots and put in a small bowl. Add the vinegar and a pinch of salt and pepper. Let sit for 15 minutes or so, then whisk in the olive oil. Taste and adjust the acid and salt as needed. Toss the dressing with the tomatoes. Add the basil leaves, either cut into thin ribbons or whole. Toss gently, taste for seasoning, and adjust as needed.

VARIATIONS:
- In place of the shallots, flavor the dressing with garlic pounded to a paste in a mortar.
- Substitute half the tomatoes with 1 pound green beans (trimmed and cooked until just tender in salted boiling water) or sliced cucumbers.

Caesar Salad

Zingy, salty, cheesy Caesar dressing is perfect for a salad of sturdy, crunchy romaine or escarole lettuce. Add chicken and sweet apples and it becomes more than a salad—it is a satisfying meal.

MAKES 8 SERVINGS

FOR THE DRESSING:
½ cup grated Parmesan cheese
1 egg yolk
Juice of 2 lemons (¼ cup)
2 garlic cloves
1 teaspoon Dijon-style mustard
½ teaspoon fresh-ground black pepper
4 anchovy fillets (optional)
½ teaspoon kosher salt
1 cup olive oil

FOR THE SALAD:
3 large heads romaine lettuce
½ loaf whole wheat bread (5 ounces)
1 tablespoon vegetable oil

To make the dressing, add all the ingredients except the olive oil to the pitcher of a blender or the bowl of a food processor. Blend until smooth. With the machine running on low speed, drizzle in the olive oil until the dressing emulsifies. Transfer the dressing to a small bowl and refrigerate until ready to dress the salad.

Prepare the lettuce: Remove any bruised or damaged outer leaves. Cut the lettuce into quarters lengthwise and then coarsely chop crosswise into bite-size pieces. Wash the lettuce in a bowl of cold water, drain, and spin-dry in a salad spinner. Refrigerate until ready to use.

Preheat the oven to 375°F.

To make the croutons, cut the crusts off the bread (save them for another use) and dice into ½-inch cubes. Put the cubes in a bowl and toss with the vegetable oil. Spread them out on a baking sheet and bake for 15 to 20 minutes, until golden and crisp all the way through. Use a spatula to turn and stir them two or three times during the baking process. When done, let cool completely.

When ready to serve, combine the lettuce, croutons, and dressing in a large bowl and toss well.

VARIATIONS:

- For a more substantial salad, substitute half the romaine lettuce with 3 boneless chicken breasts, diced and roasted. And if you like, add 1 pound or so of sliced apples.
- Pound 2 or 3 garlic cloves to a paste in a mortar and add to the vegetable oil to toss with the croutons before baking.
- Use Little Gem or escarole lettuce instead of romaine.

Apple and Cabbage Slaw

MAKES 8 SERVINGS

1 small head red cabbage
½ small head green cabbage
1 small red onion
Kosher salt

2 apples
2 tablespoons cider vinegar
Fresh-ground black pepper
½ cup olive oil

Remove and discard any tough outer leaves of the cabbages. Cut the cabbages into quarters and remove the cores. Turn cut-side down and slice crosswise into thin ribbons. Peel the onion, cut in half, and slice the halves as thin as possible. Combine the cabbage and onion in a bowl and season with salt. Cut the apples into quarters and remove the cores. Cut the quarters into thin slices and add to the cabbage and onion.

Combine the vinegar, salt, and pepper to taste, and whisk to dissolve the salt. Add the olive oil. Taste for acid and salt balance and adjust as necessary. Pour the dressing over the cabbage, onion, and apples and mix well.

VARIATIONS:

- Use red, green, savoy, and/or napa cabbage, singly or in any combination, with or without the apples.
- Stir in ¼ cup chopped fresh parsley, cilantro, or other tender herbs at the end.
- Soak the sliced onion in ice water for 10 to 15 minutes before using to temper the raw taste, if you like.

Napa Cabbage Slaw

Tender napa cabbage—lighter and lacier than green or red cabbage—makes a simple and refreshing slaw. It is especially good made with cilantro and jalapeño chiles and piled onto Chile Braised Pork Tacos (page 98).

MAKES 8 TO 10 SERVINGS

2 small heads or 1 large head napa cabbage (2 to 3 pounds)
1 small red onion
Ice water
Kosher salt

4 tablespoons rice vinegar or cider vinegar
Fresh-ground black pepper
½ cup olive oil or vegetable oil

Remove and discard any tough outer leaves of the cabbages. Cut the cabbages in half lengthwise and remove the cores; cut a large head into quarters. Turn cut-side down and slice crosswise into fine shreds. Peel the onion, cut in half, and slice the halves as thin as possible. Soak the onion in ice water for 5 to 10 minutes to soften the raw flavor; drain. Combine the cabbage and onion in a bowl and season with salt.

In a separate bowl, combine the vinegar, salt, and pepper to taste, and whisk to dissolve the salt. Add the olive oil. Taste for acid and salt balance and adjust as necessary. Pour the dressing over the cabbage and onion and mix well.

VARIATIONS:
- Stir in ½ cup chopped fresh cilantro, parsley, or other tender herbs at the end.
- Add 2 teaspoons toasted and ground cumin seeds.
- Mix in 2 thinly sliced jalapeño chiles (seeds and ribs removed for milder flavor), and substitute lime juice for the vinegar.

Shaved Carrot Salad

I look forward to the cool weather when rainbow carrots are in season to make this beautiful salad with red, yellow, light orange, and dark orange carrots, and even purple carrots with deep orange interiors. The carrots are transformed when cut into paper-thin slices that curl and tangle, and they never fail to delight children.

A mandoline* is an essential tool for slicing and shaving vegetables beautifully and efficiently.

MAKES 8 SERVINGS

2 pounds carrots
  (as many colors as available)
Zest of 1 lemon
6 tablespoons lemon juice
  (about 2 lemons)
3 teaspoons white wine vinegar or
  cider vinegar
Kosher salt and fresh-ground black
  pepper
½ cup olive oil

Peel the carrots and trim the tops and ends.

To make the dressing, combine the lemon zest and juice, vinegar, salt and pepper to taste, and olive oil. Whisk together, taste, and adjust the balance as needed.

Use a swivel-bladed vegetable peeler or a mandoline (carefully) to shave the carrots as thin as possible. Toss them in a bowl with the dressing, taste, and adjust the salt and acid as needed.

VARIATIONS:
- Make the salad with other shaved vegetables, such as cucumber, fennel, golden beets, celery, red peppers, or radishes, in any combination or singly.
- Make a shaved zucchini and summer squash salad dressed with lemon, olive oil, and herbs.
- To make the shaved carrots curl, soak them in ice water until they curl, drain and dry, and toss with the dressing.

---

*Benriner is an inexpensive and reliable brand with an adjustable blade that can be set for slices from paper-thin to ⅓ inch thick—use safely and correctly, of course.

Miso-Sesame Cucumbers

Slender, thin-skinned Persian, English, or Japanese cucumbers with few seeds are best for this salad. Make it without peeling the cucumbers or use a vegetable peeler to partially peel in lengthwise strips for a nice striped effect. Salting the cucumbers draws out watery juices and makes them pleasantly crunchy.

MAKES 6 SERVINGS

1½ pounds cucumbers
2 teaspoons kosher salt
¼ cup sesame seeds

3 tablespoons white miso
2 tablespoons rice vinegar

Slice the cucumbers into paper-thin rounds (a mandoline works very well). Combine the cucumbers and salt in a bowl or colander and let sit for 10 to 15 minutes.

Heat a small dry frying pan over medium heat. Add the sesame seeds and toast for a few minutes, until they are fragrant and begin to pop. Remove from the heat, let cool, and grind the seeds to a rough paste in a suribachi or mortar. Add the miso and vinegar and stir until creamy.

By handfuls, squeeze the cucumbers to release the water, then combine them with the miso dressing and mix well.

VARIATIONS:
- If you like, add a few shiso leaves cut into fine ribbons.
- Make a smashed cucumber salad with the same dressing: With a wooden baton or the side of a cleaver, whack the whole cucumbers to gently split them. Cut in half lengthwise and then into 2-inch pieces. Toss with the dressing and let marinate for 10 minutes or so.

Tabbouleh

Tabbouleh is a Lebanese salad made with bulgur, chopped herbs, and tomatoes—green and fresh with more herbs than grain, and robust enough that it can be assembled in advance and refrigerated overnight. Bulgur wheat is made from wheat grains that have been parboiled or steamed and then dried. It requires only soaking and dressing.

MAKES 8 SERVINGS

1 cup bulgur
2 to 3 large bunches parsley
   (1½ cups chopped)
2 bunches mint (1 cup chopped)
1 to 2 bunches scallions
   (1 cup sliced)
4 ripe medium tomatoes
   (1½ cups diced)
Juice of 2 lemons (¼ cup)
Kosher salt
½ cup olive oil

Put the bulgur in a bowl and cover with 1 inch cold water. Soak for 30 to 40 minutes to plump the grains until tender, then drain in a sieve.

Pick the leaves and tender stems from the parsley and mint and finely chop. Trim and thinly slice the scallions. Core the tomatoes and dice small. In a large bowl, combine the herbs, scallions, and tomatoes. With your hands, squeeze the soaked bulgur to remove as much water as possible, then mix it into the herbs and tomatoes.

Whisk together the lemon juice, salt to taste, and olive oil. Add to the bowl with the bulgur-tomato mixture and mix well. Taste and add more salt, lemon juice, or olive oil if needed. Let rest about 1 hour to allow the bulgur to absorb the flavors. Taste again and adjust if needed before serving.

VARIATIONS:
- If you like, serve with romaine leaves to use as scoops for eating the salad.
- Use halved cherry tomatoes in place of the larger tomatoes, or a combination of both.
- Make the salad with 2 cups cooked brown rice in place of the bulgur.

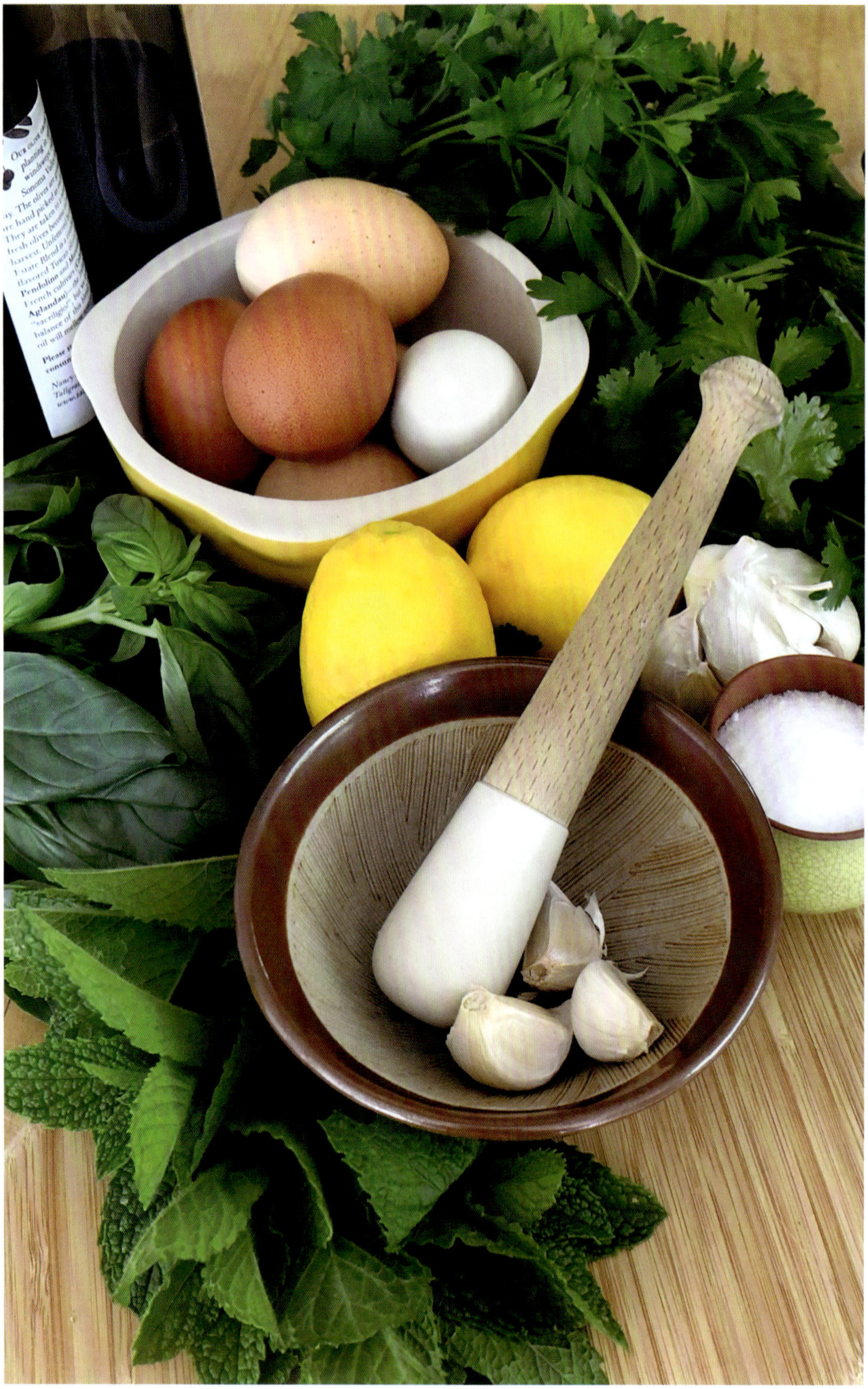

Sauces

A few simple sauces are essential to a lunch menu repertoire centered on great seasonal produce. These sauces, quick and easy to make with just a few ingredients, add wonderful flavor, color, and depth to any dish.

Vinaigrette, made with fruity olive oil and flavorful vinegar or citrus juices, is the versatile, indispensable dressing. It can turn almost any combination of vegetables into a salad. Vinaigrette can be flavored additionally with diced shallot, pounded garlic, chopped herbs, anchovy, grated cheese, mustard, and more.

Aioli—garlicky mayonnaise—is another all-purpose sauce for sandwiches, raw and cooked vegetables, meats and fish, and fried things. Make it without the garlic (or with it) and the mayonnaise can be flavored with chopped herbs, capers, pickles, mustard, miso, spices, and citrus, in whatever combinations you like.

Raita is a light tangy yogurt sauce, deliciously flavored with herbs, grated cucumbers or carrots, garlic or ginger, and/or toasted warm spices. It is especially good with rice and vegetables, falafel and flatbread, and roasted vegetables, and as a garnish for soups.

Salsa Verde brings the aromatic magic of fresh green herbs, garlic, and lemon zest. It adds brightness, freshness, and vibrant green color to any dish.

Tomato Sauce is, of course, foundational to many pasta dishes and pizza toppings. Use the best-tasting tomatoes available, whether fresh, preserved, or canned, to make a sauce with real flavor. If possible, when tomatoes are abundant and at their best, process and preserve them to stock the pantry and enhance your menus throughout the year.

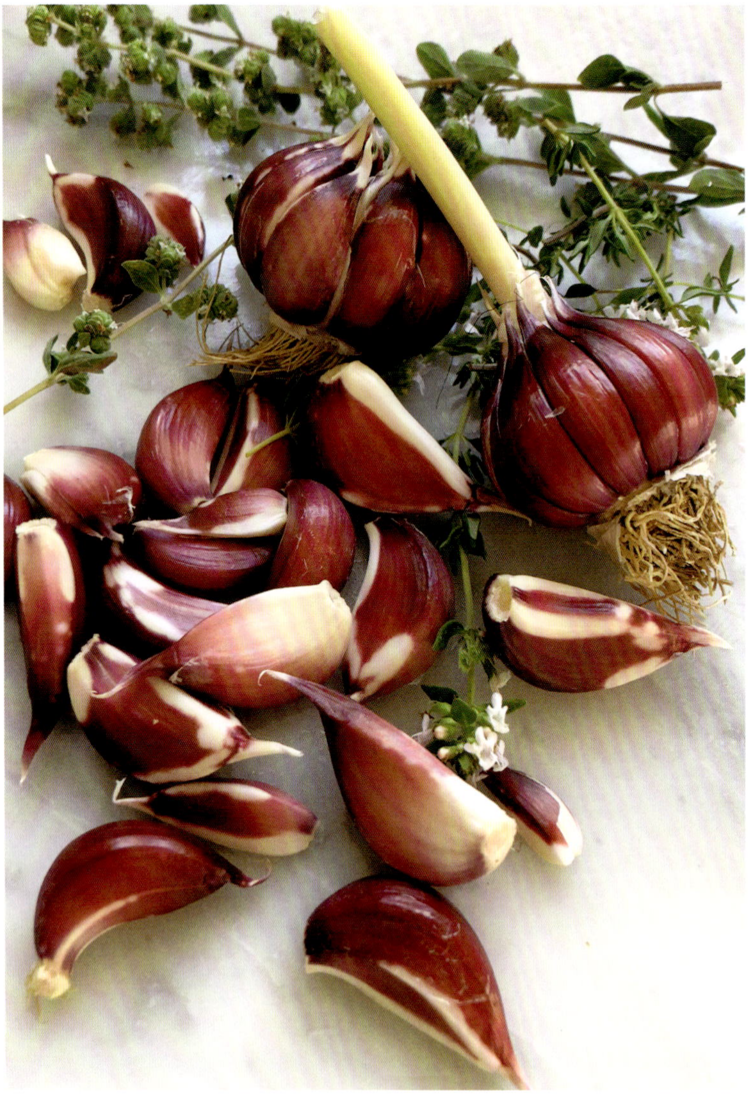

A NOTE ABOUT GARLIC

Garlic is as good as ten mothers, as the old adage goes. There is some controversy over whether that refers to the healthy beneficial qualities of garlic or to the aromatic effect it may have on potential suitors. For me, it is the former. Garlic, raw and cooked, is essential to the vegetable-centered food that I love to cook and eat every day. A freshly pounded paste of raw garlic is the base of the vinaigrette I make most for salads. And to go with the salad, I toast a slice of crusty bread, rub the warm toast with a clove of garlic, and drizzle with olive oil (another essential).

The use of a small mortar and pestle (I prefer a small grooved ceramic suribachi) is a good way to make a quick paste of raw garlic. Alternatively, hold a fork with its tines resting on a plate or on the bottom of a small bowl and rub a peeled clove rapidly back and forth against the tines, or use a microplane and grate the clove to a juicy purée.

Garlic has a long growing season, nearly nine months, typically planted in October or November and harvested in early summer. The garlic plants grow slowly in the winter and take off with the warmth of spring. Green garlic, or immature garlic, can be harvested beginning in April and May. The young garlic plants resemble leeks with tall green stalks of many layers before the cloves and bulbous ends begin to form. All parts of the green garlic can be used. It has a wonderfully aromatic flavor that is delicious in soups and stews and other vegetable preparations.

Mature heads of garlic are at their freshest and tastiest from mid-June to late fall—firm, juicy, and pungent but not bitter, mature garlic is especially delicious raw in aioli, vinaigrette, salsa verde, and other sauces. Garlic begins to change in the late fall, about the time in the growing cycle when it would begin to sprout if it were in the ground. If you cut the cloves in half, you will see the sprouting germ in the center. The germ has a bitter taste, so it is best to remove it before using the garlic.

Garlic is at its best when peeled and chopped just before using. As with onions, the juices are released when cut and quickly begin to oxidize. The longer it is exposed to the air, the more it oxidizes and develops "off" flavors. It will hold better if kept covered with oil until ready to use. Avoid using pre-peeled garlic and especially pre-chopped garlic.

Vinaigrette

The simplest vinaigrette is just three or four ingredients. Use the best-tasting, best-quality vinegar and oil that your budget allows. Vinegars vary quite a bit in flavor and acidity. To make a balanced vinaigrette, start by seasoning the vinegar with salt, then taste. The right amount of salt will tame the sharpness of the vinegar and enhance its fruity flavor without being too salty. It should taste delicious. Whisk in the oil until you taste acidity that is bright but not too sharp, and oil that is fruity but not too fatty and heavy.

MAKES 1 CUP

¼ cup red wine vinegar
½ teaspoon kosher salt
Fresh-ground black pepper
¾ cup to 1 cup olive oil

Pour the vinegar into a bowl, whisk in the salt, and add some black pepper. Taste for balance and adjust if needed. Whisk in the olive oil, a little at a time. Taste as you go and stop when it tastes right.

VARIATIONS:

- Make a garlic vinaigrette: Peel a garlic clove and pound to a paste in a mortar, or grate on a microplane. Add to the vinegar, salt, and pepper, then let marinate for a few minutes before adding the oil.
- Add a diced shallot to the vinegar, salt, and pepper. Let marinate 10 minutes or so before adding the oil.
- White wine vinegar, sherry vinegar, or lemon juice can replace some or all of the red wine vinegar.
- Stir in a bit of mustard before adding the oil.
- Chop some fresh herbs and stir them into the finished vinaigrette.

Aioli

Aioli—fresh mayonnaise flavored with pounded raw garlic—is delicious for sandwiches and as a sauce or dip for raw and cooked vegetables, potatoes, eggs, crusty bread, fish and meats, or almost anything, and kids love it.

MAKES 1 CUP

1 egg (at room temperature)
Kosher salt
1 cup mild olive oil, grapeseed oil,
 or other vegetable oil, or a blend
2 or 3 garlic cloves

Separate the egg and put the yolk, a pinch of salt, and ½ teaspoon warm water in a small bowl. (Save the white for another use.) Whisking constantly, slowly drizzle in the olive oil a few drops at a time. As the yolk absorbs the oil, the sauce will thicken (emulsify), lighten in color, and become opaque. Once it thickens you can add the oil a little faster in a stream, whisking all the while. If it gets too thick before all the oil has been incorporated (it should not be too stiff and shiny), add a few drops of water to thin it out, then continue.

Peel the garlic cloves and pound to a smooth paste in a mortar with a pinch of salt. Add the garlic paste to the mayonnaise a little at a time, tasting as you go, until the garlic flavor is as strong as you like it, but not overpowering. Taste for salt and adjust as desired.

Make aioli half an hour ahead of time to allow the flavors to marry. As with anything made with raw eggs, if you are not serving the mayonnaise within an hour, refrigerate it. Aioli tastes best the day it is made.

VARIATION:
- Make a plain mayonnaise in the same way without the garlic and finished with a few drops of vinegar or lemon juice. It can be flavored with many additions: chopped fresh herbs such as parsley, chives, tarragon, chervil, or basil, singly or in combination; miso and rice vinegar; capers; or anchovies.

Raita

Raita is the versatile cooling South Asian yogurt sauce that accompanies all kinds of rice dishes, vegetables, fish, and meats. It can be flavored simply with herbs, garlic, and spices, or with grated vegetables, singly or in combination.

MAKES 3 CUPS

1 small garlic clove, peeled
1 cup fresh mint or cilantro leaves
Kosher salt
2½ cups plain yogurt

Pound the garlic to a smooth paste in a mortar. Coarsely chop the mint or cilantro leaves, add to the mortar with a pinch of salt, and pound to a rough paste. Mix the mint and garlic into the yogurt and stir well to combine. Add more salt to taste.

VARIATIONS:
- Add different herbs, such as parsley or dill, and spices. Toasted cumin seeds and turmeric will add warm flavor and color; for heat add cayenne or chiles. For a heartier sauce, add grated raw carrots, beets, or cucumber; salt them first for 15 minutes, squeeze out excess moisture, and pat dry.
- Make a simpler raita flavored with finely grated ginger and salt, without pounded or chopped herbs.

Salsa Verde

This green sauce (not to be confused with Mexican tomatillo and chile sauce) is a simple combination of olive oil and chopped parsley flavored with lemon zest, garlic, and capers. It brings bright freshness to the plate and goes with almost anything.
MAKES 1 CUP

1 cup parsley leaves
  (about ½ cup chopped)
1 small garlic clove
1 tablespoon capers
½ teaspoon kosher salt
Fresh-ground pepper
½ cup olive oil
1 small lemon

Chop the parsley leaves. Zest the lemon. Peel the garlic and chop very fine or pound to a paste in a mortar. Rinse and drain the capers and coarsely chop. Combine the parsley, garlic, capers, and lemon zest in a bowl. Add the salt and pepper to taste, stir in the olive oil, and mix well. Taste for salt and adjust if needed. Let the sauce sit for a while before serving for the flavors to come together.

VARIATIONS:
- Other fresh herbs, or combinations of herbs, can replace part or all of the parsley: cilantro, chervil, basil, tarragon, marjoram, chives, mint, or thyme.
- Add a chopped anchovy fillet, chopped hard-cooked egg, or diced shallot.
- Add a bit of lemon juice or vinegar for a zestier sauce, but add just before serving, as the acid will cause the herbs to discolor.

Tomato Sauce

MAKES 2 QUARTS

1 yellow onion
2 garlic cloves
½ bunch basil (1 cup leaves)
3 tablespoons olive oil

A pinch of dried red chile flakes
7 to 8 cups crushed tomatoes
   (or Canned Tomatoes, page 140)
2 tablespoons kosher salt

Peel and finely dice the onion. Peel and mince the garlic. Pick the basil leaves from the stems and coarsely chop. Heat a heavy-bottomed pot over medium-low heat and add the olive oil, onion, garlic, basil, and chile flakes. Cook for 10 to 15 minutes, until the onion is tender. Add the tomatoes, salt, and 2 cups water and simmer for 20 minutes.

Store extra tomato sauce in the refrigerator for up to 1 week or freeze up to 12 months.

VARIATIONS:

- Use 3 quarts peeled and chopped fresh tomatoes in place of canned tomatoes and eliminate the water.
- In place of basil, use 1 tablespoon chopped fresh marjoram.
- If needed, add a bit of sugar to sweeten the sauce.
- Make a sauce from tomato confit: Put cored whole ripe tomatoes in a baking dish, drizzle with olive oil, season with salt, add basil leaves and a few garlic cloves, and slow-roast in a 350°F oven for about 1 hour, until lightly browned and completely tender. (For more detailed instructions, see Tomato Confit, page 141.) Purée for a smooth sauce, or crush the tomatoes.

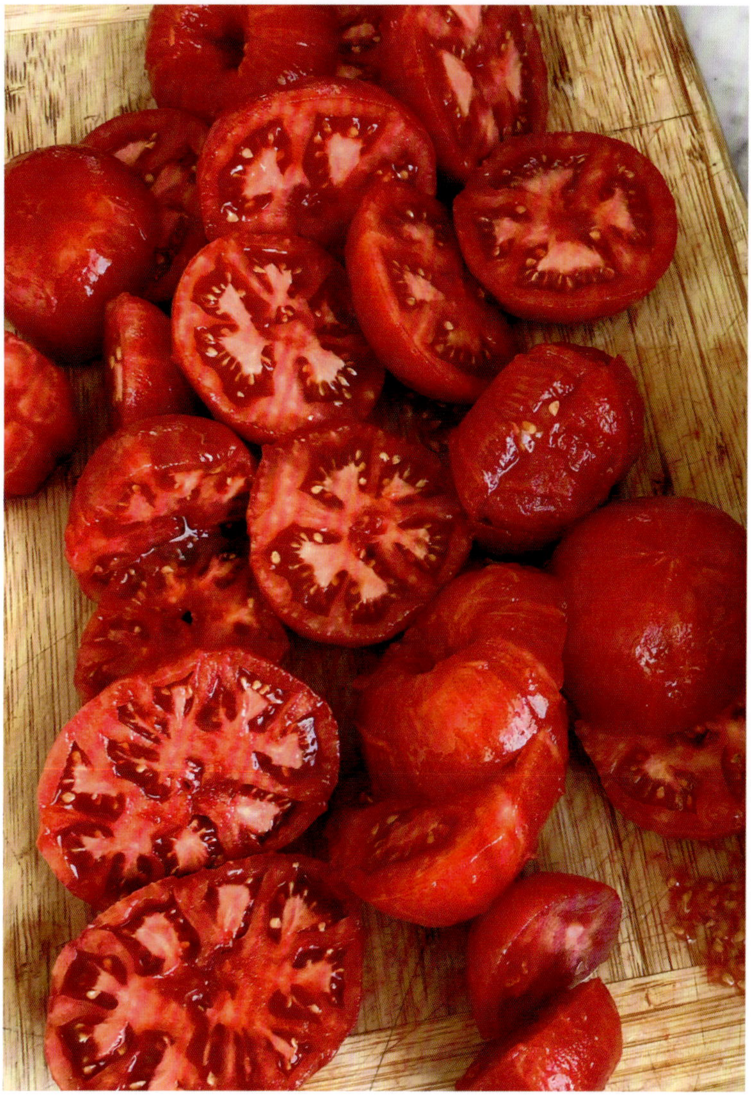

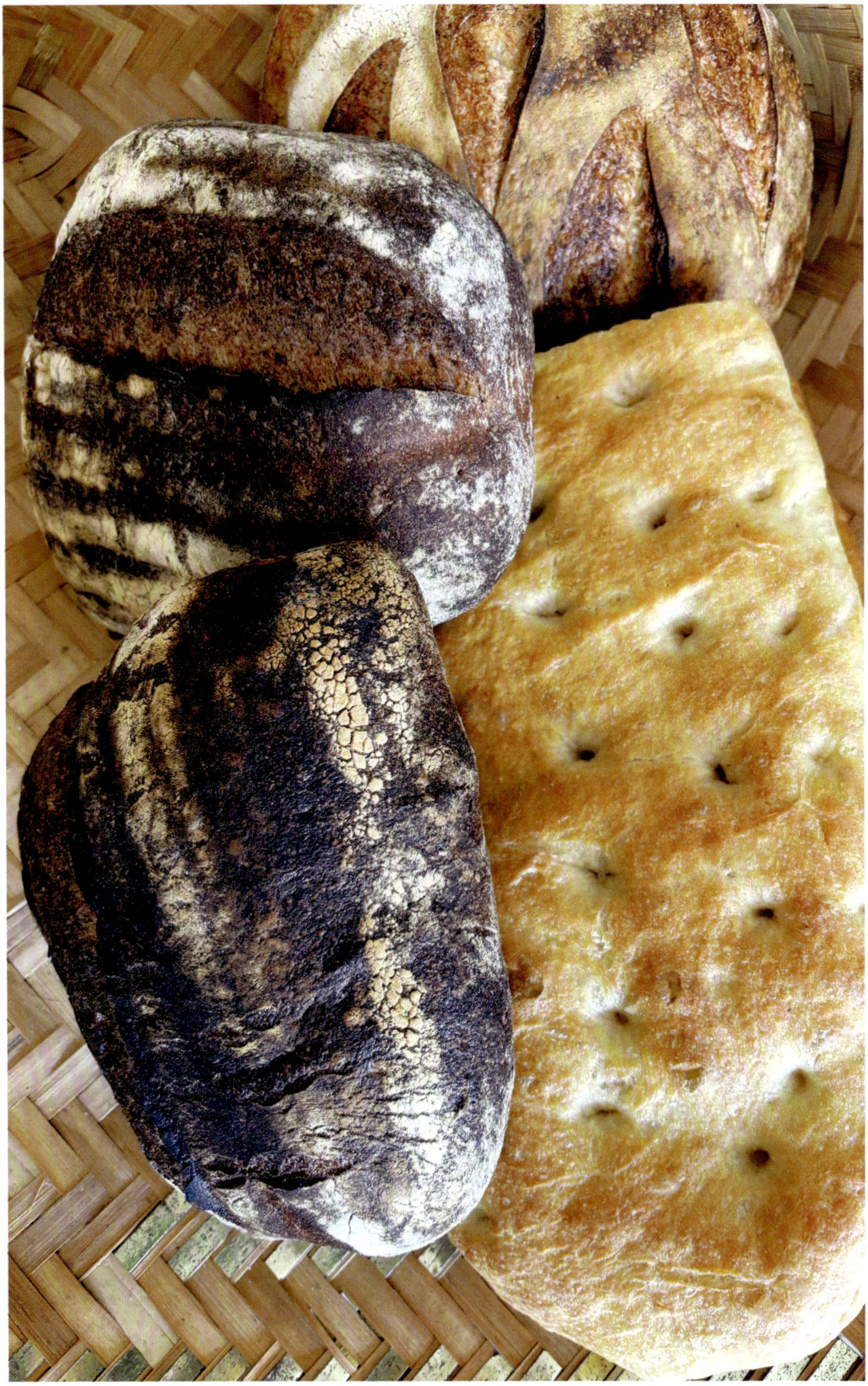

Breads and Grains

I like to imagine hungry, boisterous children rushing to their school dining hall to be greeted with the sights and smells of freshly baked stacks of pita bread, soft tortillas, golden cornbread, and yeasty focaccia. The aromas of warm bread communicate better than any description can that they are cared for, that they are deserving of good food, flavor, and beauty.

Whole grains are important sources of protein, especially if animal protein is in short supply, unavailable, or unwanted. Whole-grain flours, such as wheat, are ground from whole kernels, including the germ and bran, which makes the flour more nutritious and more flavorful. Some breads and other recipes are delicious made with all whole wheat flour, and some are better made with a combination of white and whole wheat flours for a lighter texture. Muffins and other batters are especially tasty with whole-grain flours, and make those made with white flour seem bland by comparison.

Whole grains and flours contain oils that make them more perishable than more processed white flours. If they are not to be used in quick rotation, it is better to store them in the refrigerator to keep the oils from turning rancid.

Breads, leavened or unleavened, made with a variety of grains are at the center of many food cultures. Flatbreads and pita breads are pillowy soft rounds perfect for falafel and sandwiches or for dipping in lentil dal, curries, chickpea stews, soups, hummus, and more. Thin, light focaccia has a great texture for sandwiches or topped with tomato sauce and cheese for an easy pizza. A versatile whole-grain loaf with terrific flavor is a mainstay for sandwiches and garlic toasts. Cornbread and millet muffins go with all kinds of beans and greens to soak up the flavorful juices.

Cornbread

Warm, buttery cornbread is universally loved. It combines deliciously with all kinds of beans and greens, soups, barbecue chicken, and more. It is simple to make. In a busy kitchen, the dry ingredients can be measured ahead in batches, ready to be combined with the remaining ingredients and baked just in time for lunch.

MAKES 12 SERVINGS

2½ cups cornmeal
2½ cups all-purpose flour
2½ tablespoons baking powder
2½ teaspoons kosher salt
1 cup vegetable oil or melted butter

3 eggs
¼ cup honey
2½ cups milk
2 tablespoons butter (optional)

Preheat the oven to 375°F. Line a 10-by-12-inch baking pan with sides (half hotel pan) with parchment paper.

Combine the dry ingredients in a large bowl and mix well. In a separate bowl, whisk together the vegetable oil, eggs, honey, and milk. Gently stir the wet ingredients into the dry ingredients until the batter just comes together. Pour the batter into the pan and use a spatula to spread the mixture evenly into all the corners.

Place on the middle rack of the oven and bake for 25 to 35 minutes, until cooked through. Rotate the cornbread once or twice during the baking for even coloring.

If you like, while the cornbread is still warm from the oven, rub the butter over the surface.

VARIATIONS:
- Use cornmeal made from different varieties of corn, such as blue or white.
- Bake the batter in buttered or parchment-lined muffin tins for 12 to 15 minutes.
- Add chopped jalapeño chiles, scallions, or fresh corn kernels to the batter.
- For denser cornbread, use more cornmeal in place of the all-purpose flour.

Polenta

Polenta is ground corn cooked in boiling water until thickened and tender. Although it thickens after a few minutes of cooking, long, slow simmering allows its full corn flavor to develop. It can be served soft or firm. When first cooked, soft polenta is great with sauces, vegetables, and meats such as sausage and meatballs. Cooked polenta that is allowed to cool and firm is versatile and can be cut into shapes and fried, grilled, or baked, then topped with sauce, cheese, a fried egg, sautéed vegetables, or whatever you like.

MAKES 2 QUARTS

2 quarts water
2 cups whole-grain polenta
2 teaspoons kosher salt
6 tablespoons butter or olive oil
1 cup grated Parmesan cheese
Olive oil, for baking or frying (optional)

Bring 2 quarts water to a boil in a heavy-bottomed pot. Whisk in the polenta and salt. Turn down the heat and stir constantly until the polenta is suspended in the water and no longer settles to the bottom of the pot. Cook for 1 hour, stirring occasionally, at a bare simmer. It should have a creamy, pourable consistency; add water if the polenta gets too thick.

Stir in the butter and Parmesan. Taste and add more salt if needed. (Be careful when tasting the polenta; it is very hot.) Keep warm until ready to serve—covered on very low heat or over another pan of simmering water—or spread it out on an oiled rimmed baking sheet and let cool. If you like, cut the cooled, firm polenta into triangles or other shapes, place on a sheet pan lined with parchment paper, moisten with olive oil, and reheat in a 375°F oven; or fry in a cast-iron skillet coated with olive oil.

VARIATIONS:
- Sauté 2 cups fresh corn kernels for 4 minutes, season with salt, and stir into the polenta.
- Replace the Parmesan cheese with grana, fontina, pecorino, or cheddar cheese.

Flatbread

Freshly cooked flatbreads are irresistible with all kinds of Mediterranean dips like hummus, olive oil and za'atar, and tzatziki. They also make great wraps for Falafel (page 60) or a fresh cucumber, feta, and tomato salad.

This dough is made with a combination of whole wheat flour and bread (high-gluten) flour. It can be adapted with an increase of the percentage of whole wheat flour, if you prefer, and is best made the day before you wish to use it, with a slow rise in the refrigerator overnight.

MAKES 10 FLATBREADS

1 teaspoon instant active dry yeast
1 teaspoon sugar
1½ cups cold water
¾ cup whole wheat flour
3¾ cups unbleached bread flour

2½ tablespoons olive oil
2 teaspoons kosher salt
½ cup mixed olive oil and vegetable oil

In the bowl of a stand mixer, whisk together the yeast, sugar, and water. Add both flours and 2½ tablespoons olive oil and mix with a dough hook on low speed until the dough just comes together. Add the salt and continue mixing on medium speed for 15 minutes to knead the dough into a smooth ball. Cover the bowl with plastic wrap or a lid. For the best flavor, let the dough rise 2 hours in a warm place, punch it down, cover it, and refrigerate overnight; let it come to room temperature before using. Alternatively, you can just let it rise for 4 to 5 hours in a warm place and use immediately.

Cut the dough into 10 pieces weighing about 3 ounces each. Roll the pieces into balls, place them on a baking sheet, and cover with a towel or plastic wrap. Let the balls proof (rise) for 90 minutes. When the dough balls have puffed and feel tender, roll each into a roughly 8-inch round, cover, and let rest for 20 minutes before cooking.

Heat a griddle or cast-iron pan to medium-high heat. Generously oil the bottom of the pan with some of the oil mixture and cook the flatbreads one by one, or as space allows on the griddle. Cook for 2 minutes or so on the first side, until you see the flatbread bubble and the edges start to become firm and dry. Flip and continue cooking for another 30 seconds or so, until the whole bread puffs and cooks through. Layer the cooked breads on a platter or sheet pan in a shingle pattern to cool; this allows them to cool slowly and retain moisture. Wrap the flatbreads in a clean towel to keep warm for serving, or wrap for storage and reheat later, but they are best eaten soon after cooking.

Pita Bread

The best part about homemade pita is watching them puff up like balloons when they bake. The whole wheat flour gives them an aromatic nutty flavor. They are perfect for filling or dipping into soups or hummus.

MAKES 10 TO 12 PITAS

1 teaspoon active dry yeast	2 tablespoons olive oil
1 tablespoon sugar	2½ cups whole wheat flour
1 cup plus 1 tablespoon water	1½ teaspoons kosher salt

Combine the yeast, sugar, and water in the bowl of a stand mixer and whisk until dissolved. Let the mixture rest about 20 minutes, until it begins to foam, indicating that the yeast has become active.

Add the olive oil, whole wheat flour, and salt. Using the dough hook attachment, mix the dough on medium speed for about 5 minutes, until it is smooth and has developed some elasticity. (If the dough becomes imbalanced, scrape it off the hook and continue mixing.) It will feel smooth and tacky to the touch. If mixing by hand, blend with a spoon until the dough comes together, then turn it out onto a surface lightly dusted with flour. Knead until smooth and elastic, using a minimum of flour to keep the dough from sticking. Cover the bowl with plastic wrap or a damp towel and let rest in a warm spot for 1 hour.

Portion the dough into 10 pieces. Dust them with flour so the dough does not stick to your hands, and roll them into 10 smooth balls. Sprinkle with more flour and place them on a baking tray lined with parchment paper. Cover with plastic wrap and let rise for 1 hour, or until doubled in size. Preheat the oven to 500°F. The oven needs to be as hot as possible to ensure the pitas will puff while baking.

Stretch the balls into disks, as for pizza. Dip them into flour and shake off any excess. It is important not to have excess flour on the pitas; otherwise the flour will bake on and leave a raw flavor. Cover and let rest for 5 to 10 minutes. Use a rolling pin to gently roll the disks, from the center out, into rounds about ½ inch thick and 5 to 6 inches in diameter.

While the pitas rest, place a baking sheet turned upside down in the oven to let it get very hot. (Alternatively, heat a pizza stone, if you have one and prefer it. The pitas tend to blister when baked on a stone, less so when baked on a pan.) Open the oven door and place the pitas directly on the hot baking sheet or stone. Bake until they are soft and puffed, about 4 minutes. Let cool, then reheat briefly just before serving.

Millet Muffins

Millet grains give these muffins a delicious little crunchy pop, and kids love them.
MAKES 12 MUFFINS

¾ cup millet
½ cup molasses
½ cup vegetable oil
1 egg
1½ cups whole milk

1 teaspoon cider vinegar
1¼ cups whole wheat flour
1 teaspoon baking soda
1 teaspoon baking powder
½ teaspoon kosher salt

Preheat the oven to 375°F. Grease a muffin tin with vegetable oil or line with paper muffin liners. Pulse the millet in a food processor or blender for a few seconds to slightly crack the grains.

In a bowl, beat together the molasses, vegetable oil, egg, milk, and vinegar. In a separate bowl, mix the cracked millet and all the remaining dry ingredients together. Use a rubber spatula to fold the wet ingredients into the dry ingredients until just combined. Take care not to overmix the batter.

Scoop the batter into the muffin tin, filling each cup up to the surface of the pan. Bake for 20 minutes, or until a skewer inserted in the center of a muffin comes out clean. Transfer the tin to a rack and cool to room temperature.

Focaccia

This recipe is an adaptation of the pizza bianca from the Acme Bread Company in Berkeley. It is thin and airy with a light, bubbly interior and a salty golden crust. It is great cut in half horizontally for sandwiches because of the proportion of bread to filling. It makes a delicious Roman-style pizza, topped with tomato sauce and cheese or other toppings and heated briefly in a hot oven; or slice it and serve with soups and stews for a satisfying meal.

(Note: Be sure to use *instant* active dry yeast for the recipe.)

MAKES ONE 13-BY-18-INCH BREAD

FOR THE SPONGE:

¾ cup plus 1 tablespoon room-temperature water
¼ teaspoon instant active dry yeast
1⅓ cups all-purpose flour

Make the sponge: In a bowl, whisk together the water and yeast, and add the flour to create a doughlike sponge. Cover the bowl with plastic wrap or a lid and let rise in a warm place for about 4 hours. Place in the refrigerator to continue to rise slowly overnight.

FOR THE DOUGH:

Sponge (rested and proofed)
2¼ teaspoons kosher salt
1¼ cups room-temperature water
⅛ teaspoon instant active dry yeast
4¾ cups all-purpose flour
1 tablespoon olive oil

Make the dough: Remove the sponge from the refrigerator and let it come to room temperature. Add the salt to ¼ cup water and reserve. In the bowl of a stand mixer fitted with a dough hook, combine the remaining 1 cup water, the yeast, sponge, flour, and olive oil, and mix for 3 minutes on low speed. Stop the mixer, add the reserved saltwater mixture, and let stand for 5 minutes. Mix again on low speed for 1 minute and then on high speed for 3 minutes, or until the dough comes together into a smooth, well-kneaded mass. Cover the dough and let rise in a warm place (less than 80°F) for about 6 hours.

BAKING:
¼ cup plus 2 tablespoons olive oil
1 teaspoon flaky sea salt
2 cups hot water

Oil a 13-by-18-inch half sheet pan with ¼ cup olive oil. Gather the dough into a ball, coax it into a rough rectangle, and place it in the center of the oiled pan. Press the dough out with your fingertips to fill the pan about halfway. Cover with a towel, let rest for 45 minutes, and then finish stretching the dough all the way to the edges of the pan to an even thickness. Cover again with a towel and let rise for 2 hours, or until very bubbly and puffy.

When the dough is almost done rising, preheat the oven to 480°F and place a cast-iron pan on the bottom rack of the oven. Give the dough a final "dimple" with your fingertips, drizzle with the remaining 2 tablespoons olive oil, and sprinkle with the salt. Place the focaccia on the upper rack of the oven and carefully pour the water into the cast-iron pan. Close the oven door quickly and turn the heat down to 460°F. Bake for about 20 minutes, until the crust is golden brown. Remove the pan from the oven and cool on a rack for 10 minutes. Remove the focaccia from the pan and let it finish cooling on the rack.

VARIATIONS:
- Add 1 tablespoon chopped fresh rosemary or other herbs to the final mixing stage of the dough.
- Top the unbaked, proofed dough with olives, cooked onions, tomato sauce, cheese, or other toppings, and add 5 to 10 minutes to the baking time.

Edible Schoolyard Loaf

This naturally leavened bread was created by my dear friend Steve Sullivan at Acme Bread Company after I asked him for a tasty whole-grain loaf that we could use for school lunches. The catch was that it had to be organic, high in whole grains, and something that kids would absolutely love. The result is this delicious and healthy whole-grain bread that is named for the Edible Schoolyard Project (to which Acme donates a portion of the sales).

Steve shared the recipe with us and we adapted it slightly (to 60 percent whole grain, but make it with all whole grain, if you like) for easier preparation in a non-professional bakery setting. It is a multistage process that requires a natural starter sponge in place of instant yeast, an autolyse dough step that allows whole-grain flour to fully hydrate and soften to yield a tender crumb, and multiple slow rises to develop maximum flavor.

Natural starter can be purchased, or you can make it yourself by combining flour and water (100 percent flour to 95 percent water by weight: 100 grams flour to 95 grams water) and letting it slowly ferment over several days to generate an active fermenting culture. Once established, the starter culture can be maintained with regular feeding and refreshment and temperature control (particularly if you bake frequently). A bit of online research will yield options and more information.

Although this recipe requires a greater investment of time and attention than many other whole-grain breads, the rewards are well worth the effort. It is an exceptional loaf that has structure yet is tender and moist with deep, complex flavors and a dark crust that toasts wonderfully. It is my favorite bread.

MAKES 2 LOAVES APPROXIMATELY 1¾ POUNDS EACH

FOR THE SPONGE:
2 tablespoons active natural starter
1 cup whole wheat flour
1 cup bread flour
¾ cup plus 2 tablespoons water at 75°F

Mix the sponge ingredients together in a bowl. Cover and ferment at room temperature for 4 hours. While the sponge is proofing, make the autolyse dough.

AUTOLYSE DOUGH:
2 cups whole wheat flour
2 cups bread flour
⅛ teaspoon kosher salt
½ cup plus 1 tablespoon pumpernickel flour
3 cups water at 75°F

In the bowl of a stand mixer with a paddle attachment, combine the autolyse dough ingredients until they are well mixed. Cover and let rest at room temperature for 4 hours.

FINAL DOUGH:
Sponge (rested and proofed)
1½ cups whole wheat flour
1½ tablespoons honey
Autolyse Dough (rested)
1¼ tablespoons kosher salt
1½ tablespoons water at 75°F

Add the sponge, whole wheat flour, and honey to the bowl with the autolyse dough and, using a dough hook, mix on low speed to incorporate. Let rest for 1 minute and then mix on medium speed for 4 minutes. Dissolve the salt in the water, add to the dough, and mix for another 4 minutes on medium to high speed. The dough should be at 75°F. Cover and ferment in a warm place for 45 minutes.

Moisten your hands with water, gently lift the dough mass from the bottom of the bowl, and fold it onto itself 2 or 3 times, taking care not to deflate the dough—this works to increase the dough's elasticity and tension. Cover and continue fermenting for 45 minutes; fold again 2 or 3 times and ferment 30 minutes more. Divide the dough into 2 equal pieces and, with extra flour as needed to prevent sticking, gently fold the edges up to shape 2 free-form loaves; flip them over and place them onto baking sheets, or place the loaves into loaf pans. Let rise for a final 60 minutes.

About 15 to 20 minutes before the loaves finish rising, preheat the oven to 500°F. Once they are done rising, slash the tops of the loaves to allow for expansion as they bake (a single-edge razor blade works really well). Place onto a rack in the lower part of the oven and bake for 10 minutes. Turn the oven down to 475°F and continue baking for 35 minutes more, or until the loaves have an internal temperature of 190°F and sound hollow when thumped. Let the loaves cool on a rack for at least 1 hour before serving. The bread is best eaten the day it is baked but retains its moisture for several days and freezes well.

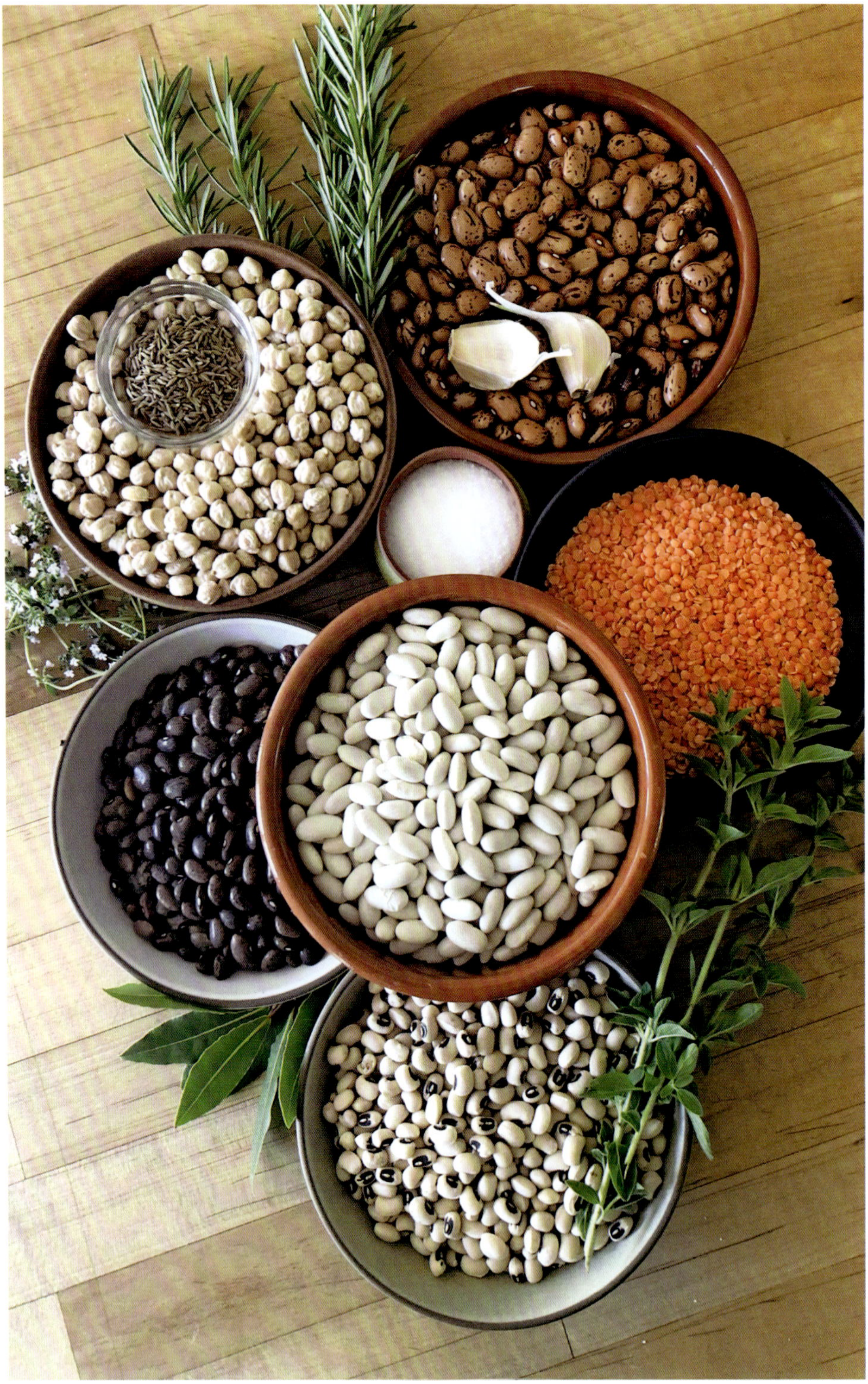

Beans and Legumes

Beans are essential to traditional foods around the globe, and for good reason. They are widely available, inexpensive, easy to store and cook, delicious, and extremely nutritious. A small sampling of basic and versatile dishes includes: beans and greens, dal and rice, bean and pasta soup, chickpeas and couscous, falafel and flatbread, hummus and vegetables, beans and tortillas.

Try to source beans from a recent harvest. They will cook more evenly and quickly and have better flavor than older beans. A simple cooking method applies to most dried beans. Cooking times vary with the variety and type of bean, and with age. If possible, soak the beans in plenty of water at room temperature for a few hours or in the refrigerator overnight. When you are ready to cook, drain the beans and cook them in a pot with a generous amount of water. Bring the beans to a boil, lower the heat, and simmer gently until tender but not falling apart. If you like, and depending on the final serving method of the beans, flavor with aromatic vegetables, herbs, chiles, and spices. When the beans are fully cooked, let them cool in their liquid.

Beans can be flavored during or at the end of their cooking and served right away, or once cooked they can be cooled, with added flavoring or not, refrigerated (or frozen) in their liquid, and used later. The cooking liquid, or broth, is flavorful and can be the basis of a delicious soup or sauce.

It is easy to scale up bean recipes for large amounts. A general guide to quantities is: 1 pound (about 2 cups) dried beans yields 6 cups cooked beans.

Cranberry Beans

Cranberry beans, or borlotti beans, are light reddish brown with dark-brown speckles. Full flavored and plump, they are a typical bean for soups such as pasta e fagioli and minestrone. They are delicious flavored with onion, tomato, and spices, especially paired with Sautéed Greens (page 112) and Cornbread (page 46).

MAKES 1½ QUARTS

2 cups dried cranberry beans (1 pound)	2 or 3 garlic cloves, minced
1 tablespoon olive oil	½ cup tomato purée
¾ cup finely diced onion	1 tablespoon cumin seeds, lightly toasted and ground
Kosher salt	2 teaspoons smoked paprika

Put the beans in a large bowl, cover with 3 quarts cold water, and place in the refrigerator to soak overnight.

When you are ready to cook the beans, drain them, pour them into a pot, and cover with 3 quarts cold water. Bring to a boil over high heat, then reduce the heat to a simmer. Skim off any foam that rises to the surface of the water.

In a separate pot, heat the olive oil over medium heat, add the onion, season lightly with the salt, and cook until softened. Add the garlic and sizzle briefly without browning. Add the tomato purée and cook until reduced a bit. Add the spices and cook 1 minute more.

Add the onion-tomato mixture to the beans. Lightly season with salt and simmer for about 2 hours, until the beans are tender and creamy but not falling apart. If needed, add more hot water during the cooking as the beans expand; they should always be submerged in the liquid. Taste and add more salt as needed.

If not serving right away, let the beans cool and then refrigerate up to 1 week, or freeze in their liquid up to 3 months.

VARIATIONS:

- In place of the onion-tomato mixture, simmer the beans with 1 small peeled carrot, 1 celery stalk, 1 small peeled onion, 1 head of garlic cut in half, and 1 bay leaf. Once the beans are cooked, remove the aromatic vegetables and bay leaf, and flavor as you like, such as with garlic, dried red chile flakes, and herbs all sizzled in olive oil.

✧ Cook other varieties of dried beans in the same way. Vary the flavorings with fresh herbs such as rosemary, thyme, sage, marjoram, and oregano, or use additional diced vegetables such as celery and carrots.

Black-Eyed Peas

Small and earthy black-eyed peas, and related varieties of cowpeas, crowder peas, and field peas, are loved and common throughout the South. Ham hocks and other pork flavorings are typically included in the cooking, but I like them even better without meat. They are naturally paired with Collard Greens (page 113) and other leafy greens. Serve with Cornbread (page 46), Brown Rice (page 73), or Millet Muffins (page 51) to mop up the tasty juices.

MAKES 2¼ QUARTS

3 cups dried black-eyed peas (1½ pounds)
1 carrot, peeled
1 celery stalk
1 onion, peeled
1 garlic head, cut in half
1 teaspoon ground cumin (optional)
1 bay leaf
1½ tablespoons kosher salt

Put the black-eyed peas in a large bowl, cover with 3 quarts cold water, and place in the refrigerator to soak overnight.

When you are ready to cook the peas, drain them and pour them into a pot. Add the carrot, celery, onion, garlic, cumin (if using), bay leaf, and salt and cover with 3 quarts cold water. Cook over high heat until boiling and then reduce the heat to a gentle simmer. Skim the foam that rises to the surface of the water, and continue cooking for 1 to 1½ hours, stirring occasionally, until the peas are completely tender. The cooking time will vary depending on the age and quality of the black-eyed peas. Remove the aromatic vegetables and bay leaf before serving, taste for salt, and adjust if needed.

Falafel

Falafel are fritters made with soaked dried chickpeas, spices, and lots of herbs. They can also be made with fava beans or a mixture of the two. In this version, the falafel are baked instead of typically deep-fried. Falafel make a great sandwich with fresh Flatbread (page 48), Raita (page 40), Pickled Red Cabbage (page 135), herby salad, or slaw.

MAKES 30 FALAFEL

1½ cups dried chickpeas
¼ yellow onion
2 garlic cloves
1 large bunch cilantro
1 large bunch Italian parsley
1 tablespoon ground cumin
¼ teaspoon baking soda
Zest and juice of 2 lemons (about 6 tablespoons juice)
1 tablespoon kosher salt
4 tablespoons olive oil

Put the chickpeas in a large bowl, cover with 4 cups cold water, and place in the refrigerator to soak overnight.

Preheat the oven to 400°F.

Cut the onion into rough chunks. Peel the garlic cloves and pick the cilantro and parsley leaves from the stems. If you like, include the small cilantro stems, which are tender and delicious.

Strain the chickpeas and put them in the bowl of a food processor along with all the other ingredients except the olive oil. Pulse until puréed and well mixed; the mixture will look slightly grainy. Taste for seasoning and add more salt or lemon juice if needed.

Use a spoon or a small ice cream scoop to form the falafel mixture into thirty 1½-ounce patties. Pour the olive oil onto a half sheet pan and spread over the pan. Spacing them evenly, place the patties on the oiled sheet pan and bake for 30 minutes. Halfway through the baking time, flip the patties over and rotate the pan. They should be golden brown on both sides when done. Place them on a dish lined with paper towels to absorb any excess oil before serving.

Yellow Lentil Dal

Dal, made with yellow, red, or other small split lentils, is an essential dish in Indian and other South Asian cuisines. A simple version made with the comforting flavors of warm spices and served with rice is for many the very taste of home. It is usually cooked to a rather thick texture but can be thinner and soupy as well. It is delicious served with warm, soft Pita Bread (page 50) to dip in the dal.

MAKES 2½ QUARTS

- 3 cups split yellow lentils (toor dal)
- 1½ cups chopped tomatoes
- 2 or 3 green chiles, halved, seeded, and sliced
- 1 teaspoon turmeric
- 1½ teaspoons kosher salt
- ¾ cup ghee (clarified butter) or coconut oil
- 1½ teaspoons cumin seeds
- 1½ teaspoons brown or black mustard seeds
- 4 to 6 garlic cloves, minced
- ½ onion, finely chopped
- 1 recipe Pita Bread (page 50)

Pick over the lentils to remove any small stones, then rinse thoroughly. Put the lentils in a pot and add the tomatoes, chiles, turmeric, salt, and 3 quarts cold water. Bring to a boil over high heat, then reduce the heat and gently simmer until the lentils have softened, about 25 to 30 minutes. Use an immersion blender to purée about half the dal (or pass it through a sieve or use a food processor), then return it to the pot. Continue to simmer, stirring occasionally, until the dal is very soft and tender, about 30 minutes. Taste for salt and adjust if needed.

Just before serving, prepare the sizzle, or tadka, as it is called in Indian cooking. Heat a small heavy-bottomed pan over medium-high heat. When it is hot, add the ghee, cumin and mustard seeds, garlic, and onion. Cook until the garlic just begins to color and the seeds begin to crackle. Pour over the dal. Serve immediately with warm pita or long-grain rice.

VARIATIONS:
- Add a few curry leaves and/or cinnamon bark to the sizzle for more aromatic flavor.
- Substitute red lentils for the yellow lentils.

Hummus

Hummus is a deliciously simple purée of cooked chickpeas, tahini, garlic, and lemon. It originated in the Middle East, where it is a versatile spread for pita pockets and sandwiches, or a dip for crisp raw vegetables. A traditional meze plate is hummus with a beautiful array of vegetables such as carrots, radishes, sweet peppers, celery stalks, cucumbers, romaine or Little Gem lettuce leaves, and fennel slices alongside green olives and crackers.

MAKES 1½ QUARTS

2 cups dried chickpeas (1 pound)
½ carrot
½ onion
½ celery stalk
1 bay leaf
1 tablespoon kosher salt
1 teaspoon garlic pounded to a paste

Juice of 1 lemon
    (about 3 tablespoons)
2 tablespoons olive oil
¾ teaspoon ground cumin (optional)
½ cup tahini (optional;
    see Variations)

Put the chickpeas in a bowl, cover with 1½ quarts cold water, and place in the refrigerator to soak overnight.

When you are ready to cook the chickpeas, drain them and pour them into a pot. Add the carrot, onion, celery, bay leaf, and salt and cover with 1½ quarts cold water. Bring to a boil over high heat, then reduce the heat to a gentle simmer. Cook for 1½ to 2 hours, stirring occasionally, until the chickpeas are completely tender.

Strain the chickpeas, reserving 2 cups of the cooking liquid, and discard the bay leaf and aromatic vegetables (or purée the vegetables in the hummus!). Let the chickpeas cool for several minutes.

Put the chickpeas in a food processor and add the garlic, lemon juice, olive oil, cumin (if using), tahini (if using), and 1 cup reserved cooking liquid. Blend until the hummus is completely smooth, adding more cooking liquid as needed. Taste for seasoning and add more salt or lemon juice if needed.

VARIATIONS:
- If you don't have tahini (a paste made from sesame seeds), make the hummus without it; just add more olive oil.
- Serve with a drizzle of olive oil and Marash pepper.
- To cook chickpeas for use in other dishes, follow the first part of the recipe and omit the puréeing steps.

beans and legumes

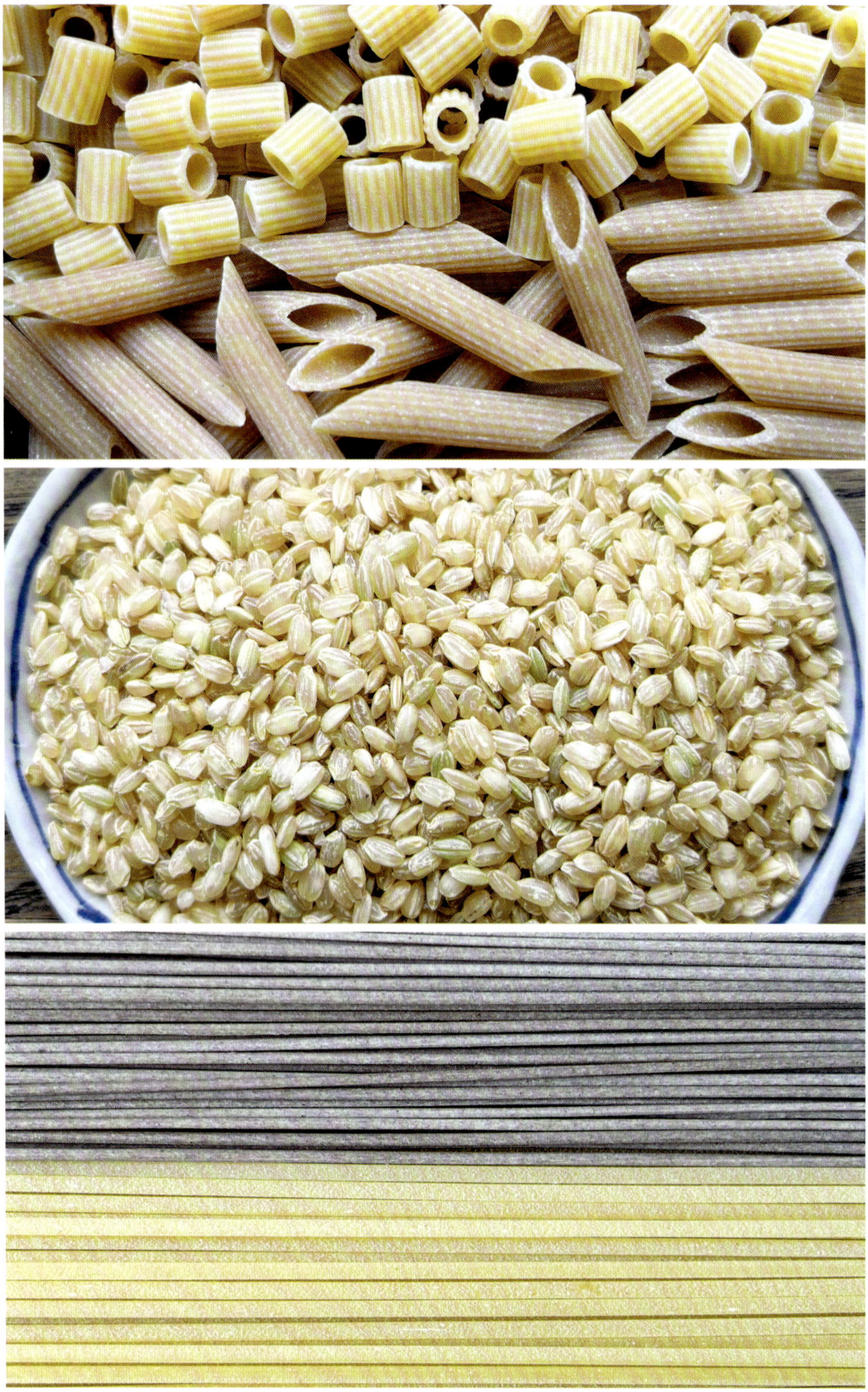

Noodles and Rice

Noodles and pasta are the ultimate partners for sauces, vegetables, cheese, and soup. Thin pasta, such as spaghetti, is delicious coated with bright pesto and served on a bed of sliced tomatoes. Broken wide noodles added to chicken soup make it into a satisfying meal. Rice noodles make a light, refreshing salad with crisp raw vegetables and a soy-sesame dressing. Couscous, although not a noodle, is made from pasta-like wheat dough in yet another variation on the theme of nutritious wheat staples.

Rice—humble, nutritious, comforting, filling, economical—is the heart and soul of many cultures. Sometimes it is the star of the menu; sometimes it plays a supporting role. There are hundreds of varieties generally divided into short-grain or long-grain categories, white or brown. Most of the recipes here call for organic brown rice because of the greater nutritional value of rice with the outer bran layer left intact. It has a nutty flavor and slightly chewy texture and requires longer cooking time than white rice.

Rice can be cooked simply by either the absorption method or the boiling method. To cook rice by the absorption method, measure the specific amounts of rice and water into a pot (add salt and butter or olive oil, if you like), bring to a boil, turn down to a simmer, cover the pot tightly, and cook the rice until all the water is absorbed, about 40 minutes for brown rice and 15 to 20 minutes for white. Let it rest, covered, for 5 to 10 minutes before fluffing and serving.

To cook rice by boiling, for each cup of rice bring about a quart of salted water to a boil. Add the rice and cook at a rapid boil until tender but not mushy—30 to 40 minutes for brown rice, 10 to 12 minutes for white rice. When cooked, drain the rice well and toss with a bit of butter or olive oil.

Another method of cooking rice, a combination of the absorption and boiling methods, works well for large quantities: Boil rice in a generous amount of lightly salted water for 6 to 7 minutes for white rice, 20 minutes or so for brown rice, until almost tender; drain and return to the pot (or hotel pan for a large amount), add butter or oil, cover tightly, and bake in a 375°F oven for an additional 15 to 20 minutes for white rice, 20 to 30 minutes for brown rice. This makes relatively dry, fluffy rice that can be kept nicely warm.

Pesto Pasta and Tomatoes

Zesty pesto brings together pasta and juicy raw tomatoes. Early Girl tomatoes have a firm texture and a tasty balance of acid and sweetness. Use another variety of tomato that is ripe, juicy, and not too soft in place of the Early Girls. Or use halved cherry tomatoes (Sungolds are delicious).

MAKES 8 TO 10 SERVINGS

2 pounds Early Girl tomatoes
Basil and Sunflower Seed Pesto (page 68)
2 tablespoons kosher salt
1½ pounds dried spaghetti
Parmesan cheese (optional)

Core the tomatoes and slice into rounds or wedges—a combination of the two shapes is visually appealing.

Put the pesto in a bowl large enough to hold the pasta spaciously with room to toss.

In a large pot, heat 4 quarts cold water to boiling and add the salt. Add the pasta and cook, stirring occasionally, until tender, about 10 minutes.

Drain the pasta, reserving 1 cup or so of cooking water, and immediately toss with the pesto. Add cooking water as needed to help mix it all together and keep it loose.

Place tomato slices around each plate and a mound of the pasta in the center. If you like, grate Parmesan over the top.

VARIATIONS:
- Spaghettis made from different grains, such as quinoa, brown rice, whole wheat, and semolina, are possible alternatives to the pasta.
- Long thin green beans (filet beans), boiled briefly until tender, or roasted sliced zucchini are delicious additions.

Basil and Sunflower Seed Pesto

This is a traditional method of making pesto, but with sunflower seeds in place of pine nuts or walnuts. It can also be made with other flavorful greens in place of basil.

MAKES 1 QUART

3 bunches basil (3 cups leaves)
Ice water
1 cup grated Parmesan cheese
2 or 3 garlic cloves, peeled
1 teaspoon kosher salt
1 cup olive oil
1 cup hulled sunflower seeds

Pick the basil leaves from the stems. Bring 2 quarts water to a boil in a large pot. Place ice water in a bowl large enough for a basket strainer to be fully submerged. When the water is boiling, add the basil and blanch for 30 seconds. Drain quickly into the basket strainer and dunk it into the ice water for a minute or two, until completely cold. This step ensures the color of the basil will remain bright and green. Remove the basket strainer from the ice water and squeeze the basil dry.

In the pitcher of a blender, combine the basil, Parmesan, garlic, salt, olive oil, sunflower seeds, and 3 tablespoons cold water. Pulse until the pesto starts to come together, then purée on high speed until smooth. Transfer to a bowl until ready to use.

VARIATIONS:
- Substitute parsley or rocket for some or all of the basil.
- Substitute grated pecorino cheese for half of the Parmesan.
- Use walnuts instead of sunflower seeds.

Chicken Noodle Soup

MAKES 2½ QUARTS

1 half chicken, or 1 leg and 1 breast on the bone
2 quarts water or chicken broth
1 medium onion, peeled and sliced, plus ½ cup diced
1 carrot, peeled and sliced, plus ½ cup diced
1 celery stalk, trimmed and sliced, plus ½ cup diced
1 large thyme sprig
2 or 3 parsley sprigs
Kosher salt
2 ounces fettuccine, broken or cut into bite-size pieces
¼ cup diced parsnip (optional)
2 teaspoons chopped fresh dill

Combine the chicken and water in a large pot. Bring to a boil and then turn down to a simmer. Skim any foam from the top of the liquid. Add the sliced onion, carrot, and celery, and the thyme and parsley sprigs. Cook at a gentle simmer for 40 minutes. Turn the burner off, carefully lift the chicken out of the broth, and let cool. Strain the broth through a fine-mesh strainer, discard the vegetables, and skim off the fat. Season generously with salt to taste, enough to bring out the full flavor of the chicken.

When the chicken is cool, remove the skin and any bones and shred the meat into bite-size pieces. Put the meat in a bowl and cover with a spoonful or two of broth to keep it from drying.

Meanwhile, bring a pot of salted water to a rapid boil. Cook the pasta until tender, then drain in a colander and rinse in cold water.

Put the diced onion, carrot, celery, and parsnip (if using) in a heavy stockpot. Cover with 4 cups of the chicken broth and cook at a gentle simmer until tender, about 15 minutes. Once the vegetables have finished cooking, add the remaining broth, the cooked noodles, and the shredded chicken. Bring to a simmer, taste, and adjust the salt as needed. Just before serving, stir in the chopped dill.

VARIATIONS:
- Garnish with fresh parsley, cilantro, or other tender herbs in place of the dill.
- Add other diced vegetables, such as leeks, potatoes, squash, celery root, turnips, and rutabagas.
- Substitute fresh noodles for dried fettuccine, or use other shapes of dried pasta.
- Substitute cooked brown rice for the noodles.

Rice Noodle Salad

This all-in-one salad has everything—noodles, vegetables, chicken, and a bright soy-sesame dressing.

MAKES 10 SERVINGS

1 tablespoon plus ½ teaspoon kosher salt	1 small head romaine lettuce
1 pound chicken tenders	4 scallions
1 pound brown rice noodles	1 bunch cilantro
2 tablespoons vegetable oil, plus more for drizzling	2-inch piece ginger
	2 tablespoons soy sauce
2 carrots	1 teaspoon toasted sesame oil
2 small cucumbers	2½ tablespoons rice vinegar
¼ small head red cabbage	2 tablespoons toasted sesame seeds
	Crackers or toasted pita (optional)

In a medium-size pot, bring 2½ quarts water to a boil. Add 1 tablespoon salt and reduce the heat to a simmer. Add the chicken tenders and poach for 15 minutes, or until cooked through. Remove from the water and let cool. Bring the water back to a boil and stir in the noodles. Boil for 10 minutes, or until tender; they should still have a springy bite to them and not be soft all the way through. Strain the noodles and rinse under cold water. Drizzle with a little vegetable oil and spread out on a sheet tray so they don't stick together.

Peel the carrots and thinly slice them lengthwise, on a slight bias, into 3-inch-long slices. Lay the slices face down and then cut lengthwise into thin matchsticks. Cut the cucumbers into matchsticks in the same manner. Cut the red cabbage and lettuce in half lengthwise, remove the cores, and cut crosswise into fine shreds. Slice the scallions into thin slivers on a slight bias. Roughly chop the cilantro, including the stems. Combine the vegetables and cilantro in a large mixing bowl.

For the dressing, grate the ginger on a microplane or on the small holes of a box grater. Use a knife to mince the grated ginger and cut up any fibrous strands. Put the ginger in a small bowl and add the soy sauce, 2 tablespoons vegetable oil, sesame oil, rice vinegar, ½ teaspoon salt, and sesame seeds. Mix well, taste for seasoning and balance, and adjust with more salt or vinegar as needed.

When the chicken is cool, use your hands to shred the tenders into bite-size pieces. Add the chicken and rice noodles to the bowl of vegetables and pour in the dressing. Toss well to combine; let sit for a few minutes before serving, for the flavors to come together. If you like, serve with crackers or toasted pita cut into long rectangles.

VARIATIONS:
- Poach chicken breasts in place of the tenders until cooked through.
- Make a vegetarian salad, without the chicken.
- Garnish with mint leaves and/or Thai basil.

Couscous

Couscous is made from semolina wheat paste shaped into small, rounded granules. It is similar in taste to dried pasta but quick-cooking, fluffy, and tender. Like rice, it serves as an accompaniment to saucy and flavorful vegetables and stews.
MAKES 8 SERVINGS

1 teaspoon kosher salt
3 cups whole wheat couscous

Bring 3½ cups water and the salt to a boil in a medium-size saucepan. Stir in the couscous and tightly cover with a lid. Remove from the heat and let steam for 5 minutes. Use a fork to fluff the couscous and break up any clumps. Serve hot right away, or keep warm, covered, over a pan of simmering water.

VARIATIONS:
- Plump ½ cup currants in a little hot water, drain, and add to the cooked couscous.
- The simplest and quickest way to cook couscous is to boil it, but for more flavor and softer texture it can be steamed, with or without aromatics such as ginger, garlic, herbs, and spices.

Fried Rice

Fried rice is a great way to combine a colorful and crunchy variety of vegetables in one dish. Change the quantities and selection as you like or have available. It's hard to go wrong whatever you choose!

MAKES 8 SERVINGS

2 carrots
4 baby bok choy
¼ head green cabbage
1 cup frozen or fresh peas
2 heads broccoli
1 tablespoon kosher salt
1 bunch scallions
¼ bunch cilantro

1-inch piece ginger
2 garlic cloves
3 eggs
4 tablespoons vegetable oil
6 cups Brown Rice (page 73)
1 tablespoon toasted sesame oil
1½ tablespoons tamari

Prepare the vegetables: Peel the carrots and trim the tops and tips. Slice them lengthwise into ¼-inch-thick strips and then cut crosswise on a bias into matchsticks.

Cut the bok choy and cabbage into thin ribbons slightly larger than the carrots, as they will shrink when cooked. Combine the carrots, bok choy, cabbage, and peas in a bowl.

Remove the core stem from the broccoli and separate the head into bite-size florets. Bring 3 quarts water to a boil in a pot. Add the salt and let dissolve. Add the broccoli and boil for 2 to 3 minutes, until just tender, and drain.

Trim the scallions and slice into thin rounds. Pick the cilantro leaves from the stems and chop fine. Place the scallions and cilantro in a separate bowl and set aside. Peel the ginger and garlic and chop fine.

Crack the eggs into a bowl and whisk together with ½ cup water. Heat a nonstick pan over medium heat and add 1 tablespoon vegetable oil. When the oil is hot, add the eggs to the pan. Do not stir until the egg has set and slightly browned on the bottom. Flip the egg over and briefly cook the other side. Slide it out onto a cutting board and let it cool slightly. Slice into thin strips about 1½ inches long.

Heat a wok or a heavy skillet over high heat and add the remaining 3 tablespoons vegetable oil, ginger, and garlic. Let sizzle for 1 minute without browning and then add the carrots, bok choy, cabbage, peas, and broccoli. Cook over very high heat, tossing frequently, for 2 to 3 minutes. Add the cooked rice, sesame oil, and tamari. Continue to cook and stir over high heat until the rice begins to fry. Stir in the egg, and when it is hot, toss in the scallions and cilantro at the very end, and serve right away.

Brown Rice

MAKES 6 CUPS

3 cups brown rice
1½ teaspoons kosher salt
1 tablespoon olive oil

Put the rice, 6 cups water, and 1 teaspoon salt in a pot and bring to a boil. Tightly cover with a lid and reduce the heat to a simmer. Cook for 40 to 45 minutes, until the rice is tender and cooked through. Remove from the heat, fluff with a fork, cover, and allow to steam for another 10 minutes. Before serving, toss the rice with the olive oil and the remaining ½ teaspoon salt.

VARIATIONS:
- If you like, cook other grains, such as quinoa or barley, separately and then fold into the warm rice.
- Substitute other whole-grain rice: red, basmati, and many more. Adjust cooking times accordingly.

Carrot and Cucumber Sushi

Nori, paper-thin dried sheets of red algae seaweed, is familiar to all sushi lovers. It is easy and fun to make sushi without a bamboo mat by simply hand rolling.
MAKES 20 ROLLS

5 cups water
2½ cups brown rice
¼ cup seasoned rice vinegar, or
 ¼ cup unseasoned rice vinegar plus 1 teaspoon kosher salt and 1 tablespoon sugar

2 large carrots
2 small, tender cucumbers
10 sheets nori (or 20 half size)
1¼ cups tamari

Bring the water to a boil and stir in the brown rice. Cover with a tight-fitting lid, turn the heat down to low, and cook for 40 minutes. When the rice is cooked, turn it out into a bowl and drizzle the vinegar over the rice. Gently stir with a wooden paddle, using a cutting action, until the rice is evenly coated. Let cool before using.

Peel the carrots. Use the julienne blade on a mandoline and shred the carrots and cucumbers into matchsticks, or cut by hand. Set aside until ready to assemble the rolls.

To assemble the rolls, cut the sheets of nori in half if using full-size sheets and lay them on the counter horizontally. Spread each piece of nori evenly with a thin layer of rice, leaving ½ inch or so of the far edge bare. In the center of each sheet, put some of the shredded carrots and cucumbers across the middle. Brush the bare edge of the nori with a little water and roll each of the sheets up tightly from the opposite side, securing with the moistened edge. Cut the rolls in half. Serve with a small dish of tamari for dipping.

VARIATIONS:
- Cook short-grain Japanese-style white rice instead of brown rice: Rinse 2 cups rice in a few changes of cold water. Drain and place in a pot with 2½ cups water. Cover the pot with a tight-fitting lid, bring to a boil, and reduce the heat immediately to low. Cook for 15 minutes. Turn off the heat and let the rice sit for another 10 minutes. Finish with seasoned vinegar as described.
- Make the rolls with ingredients such as avocado, radish sprouts, or other vegetables.
- Serve with wasabi and pickled ginger, if you like.

Chicken Congee

Congee is a traditional Chinese breakfast dish made by cooking rice until it breaks down to a porridge-like texture; it can be flavored with sweet or savory additions. It is a nutritious and comforting staple, especially for children. This savory version pairs well with Baby Bok Choy and Tamari Sauce (page 107).

MAKES 8 SERVINGS

2 skinless chicken breast fillets (6 to 8 ounces each)
1 tablespoon plus 1 teaspoon kosher salt
1-inch piece ginger, peeled and coarsely chopped
2½ cups short-grain brown rice
4 scallions

Bring 5 quarts cold water to a boil in a large pot. Reduce the heat to a simmer, add the chicken breasts, and gently poach for 15 to 20 minutes, or until cooked through with an internal temperature of 165°F. Remove the chicken from the poaching liquid and let cool. When cool enough to handle, shred the chicken into bite-size pieces and season lightly with 1 teaspoon salt. Divide into 8 equal portions.

Add the remaining 1 tablespoon salt, the ginger, and the rice to the poaching liquid and bring to a boil. Stir, reduce the heat to a low simmer, and tightly cover with a lid. Cook the rice for 2 hours or longer, stirring every 15 minutes or so, until it is very soft and thick like oatmeal.

Thinly slice the scallions. Spoon the congee into 8 bowls and top each with a little pile of the shredded chicken and scallions. Serve with baby bok choy (page 107) or steamed broccoli florets for dipping.

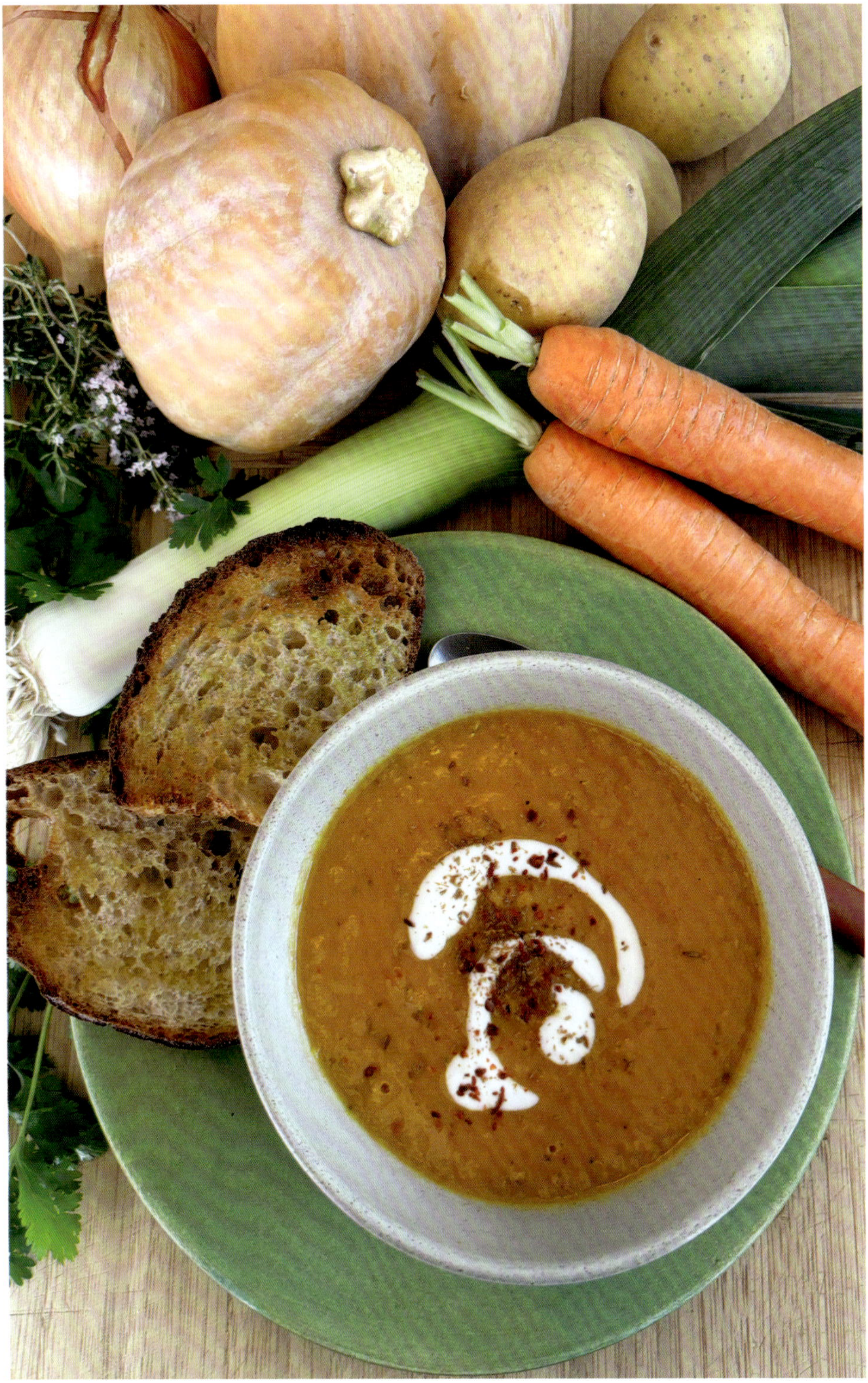

Soups

Vegetables, particularly winter vegetables, make wonderful puréed soups—sweet winter squash, carrots, rutabagas, celery root, parsnips, cauliflower, and leeks, as well as corn, tomatoes, dried beans, and lentils. They are colorful, with smooth body and texture, and do not require broth or stock because they are flavorful when made with water. Tasty garnishes add a bright touch: a swirl of cream, sour cream, or yogurt flavored with citrus zest, spicy chiles, warm spices, or fresh herbs. Soups are good accompanied with garlic toast, various breads spread with herbed cheese or wilted greens, or a grilled cheese sandwich.

Minestrone-type soups of beans, vegetables, and pasta are always satisfying and can be adapted to any season. Served with a spoonful of bright pesto or a drizzle of olive oil and cheese, and crusty garlic bread to dip in, it is a complete meal. Hearty soups such as pozole are also a meal in themselves.

Soups can be made ahead and keep well—many improve in flavor—and can help with time management and preparation time.

Butternut Squash Soup

Winter squash keeps well for months after harvesting and is a mainstay of fall and winter menus. It is delicious roasted, puréed, baked in gratins, and simmered in soups. Sweet and earthy butternut squash, with its smooth texture and deep color, makes a beautiful golden soup.

MAKES 4½ QUARTS

1 yellow onion
2 tablespoons olive oil
1 tablespoon plus 1 teaspoon kosher salt

3 pounds butternut squash
3 tablespoons butter

Peel and thinly slice the onion and put in a pot with the olive oil, 1 teaspoon salt, and ½ cup water. Cook gently over medium-low heat, stirring occasionally, until the onion is completely tender, about 10 to 15 minutes.

Peel the squash, cut in half, and remove the seeds. Coarsely dice the squash and add it to the onion along with 3 quarts cold water and the remaining 1 tablespoon salt. Bring to a boil and then immediately reduce the heat to a simmer. Cook until the squash is soft and falls apart easily when smashed on the side of the pot with a wooden spoon.

Add the butter and purée the soup in batches in a blender until completely smooth. (Be careful not to fill the blender more than halfway, use a towel to cover the lid, and make sure the lid is vented to allow the steam to escape.) Return the soup to the pot and gently reheat before serving. Taste for salt and adjust if needed.

VARIATIONS:

- Use other sweet winter squashes and/or pumpkins in combination with or in place of the butternut.
- If you like, garnish the soup with toasted and lightly crushed coriander, cumin, or fennel seeds and olive oil. Or briefly shallow-fry sage leaves in olive oil until crisp, drain, and crumble over the soup.
- Use the same method to make other vegetable soups such as carrot, rutabaga, parsnip, and more.

Corn Soup

This is a simple soup with the singular flavor of sweet corn, so *fresh* corn is key. It is especially good with colorful and tasty garnishes.
MAKES 4½ QUARTS

7 ears sweet corn
1 yellow onion
2 tablespoons olive oil
1 tablespoon kosher salt

Shuck the corn and use a towel to rub away the silk. Cut the kernels off the cobs and set aside. (To cut the kernels from the cob, hold on to the stem end, pointing the tip of the ear down, and run your knife down the cob. If you like, rub the cob with the back of the knife to collect the corn milk from the kernel bits left behind.)

Peel the onion, cut in half, and slice thin. Heat a soup pot over medium heat and add the olive oil and onion. Reduce the heat and cook the onion, stirring frequently, until tender, about 10 minutes. Add the corn, 4 quarts cold water, and salt.

Bring the soup to a simmer and cook gently for 15 minutes, or until the corn is tender. Transfer to a blender and purée in batches. Blend thoroughly so that the soup is completely smooth and emulsified. (Be careful not to fill the blender more than halfway, use a towel to cover the lid, and make sure the lid is vented to allow the steam to escape.) When the soup is smooth, return it to the pot and heat to a simmer. Taste and adjust for salt as needed.

VARIATION:
- If you like, garnish the soup with a swirl of roasted tomato or red pepper purée; a dollop of yogurt with toasted cumin seeds; basil or other tender herbs; chopped chiles or tomato salsa; or squash blossoms cut into ribbons.

Minestrone

Minestrone is a big vegetable soup that is adaptable for all seasons. A soffritto of aromatic vegetables forms the soup base with added broth or water, tender vegetables and greens, and separately cooked beans and pasta. Spring minestrone might include fresh garlic, peas, and spinach. Summer minestrone might include summer squash, green beans, tomatoes, and chard, and in winter, turnips, butternut squash, kohlrabi, potatoes, and cabbage. Almost any variation on the basic method makes a delicious soup.

Minestrone is especially good served with a dollop of Kale Pesto (page 83) and Garlic Toasts (page 83).

MAKES 2½ QUARTS

1 medium leek
1 fennel bulb
2 garlic cloves, peeled
2 carrots, peeled
1 onion, peeled
1 celery stalk, trimmed
1 bay leaf
½ teaspoon chopped fresh thyme or rosemary leaves
3 tablespoons olive oil
¾ cup tomato purée (optional)
2 cups coarsely chopped Swiss chard leaves
1 tablespoon plus 1 teaspoon kosher salt
2½ cups Cannellini Beans (page 82)
½ cup dried whole wheat pasta

Trim the root end and the tough darker greens from the leek. Cut the leek in half lengthwise and rinse well under cold water. Cut each half down the middle, and then crosswise into ¼-inch slices.

Remove and discard any brown or bruised outer layers of the fennel bulb and rinse the bulb. Slice in half and then cut into ¼-inch dice as you would an onion. Mince the garlic and dice the carrots, onion, and celery into ¼-inch cubes.

Heat a soup pot over medium heat. Add the leek, fennel, garlic, carrots, onion, celery, bay leaf, thyme, and olive oil, and cook gently, stirring often, for 5 minutes. Add the tomato purée (if using) and cook another 5 minutes. Add 1½ quarts water (or a combination of water and bean cooking liquid), the chard, and 1 tablespoon salt and simmer for 30 minutes. Add the cannellini beans and let simmer very gently.

While the soup simmers, cook the pasta. Bring 4 cups water and the remaining 1 teaspoon salt to a boil. Stir in the dried pasta and boil until almost cooked through;

it should be a little underdone. Strain the pasta in a colander and add to the soup. Continue to simmer briefly to blend all the flavors, then taste for salt and adjust if needed.

VARIATIONS:
- Serve with basil or rocket pesto in place of kale pesto, or serve with a drizzle of olive oil and grated Parmesan cheese instead of pesto.
- Substitute cranberry beans or other flavorful beans for the cannellini.

Cannellini Beans

MAKES 1½ QUARTS

2½ cups dried cannellini beans (1¼ pounds)
1 carrot, peeled
1 onion, peeled
1 celery stalk
1 head garlic, cut in half
1 bay leaf
1½ tablespoons kosher salt

Put the beans in a large bowl, cover with 3 quarts cold water, and place in the refrigerator to soak overnight.

When you are ready to cook the beans, drain them and pour them into a pot. Add the carrot, onion, celery, garlic, bay leaf, and salt and cover with 3 quarts cold water. Cook over high heat until they come to a boil, then reduce the heat to a gentle simmer. Skim the foam that rises to the surface of the water and continue cooking for 1 to 2 hours, stirring occasionally, until the beans are completely tender. Before serving, remove the aromatic vegetables and bay leaf.

VARIATIONS:
- Flavor the beans with a soffritto (a base of aromatic vegetables and herbs): Gently cook minced garlic and chopped herbs such as rosemary, sage, thyme, savory, or marjoram, singly or in combination, in a generous amount of olive oil, until soft and fragrant. Add finely diced onion and celery, if you like. Add cooked beans to the soffritto, reserving the bean liquid, and simmer gently to combine the flavors. Add the bean liquid in small amounts as needed to keep the beans loose and juicy.
- Alternatively, flavor the beans by heating 2 tablespoons olive oil over medium heat, adding 1 diced onion, seasoning lightly with salt, and cooking until softened. Add 2 or 3 minced garlic cloves and sizzle briefly without browning. Add ¾ cup tomato purée, 1 teaspoon smoked paprika, and 2 teaspoons lightly toasted and ground cumin seeds, cook until reduced a bit, and add to the beans at the start of cooking.
- Add the cooked beans to soups or pasta dishes.
- To store, let the beans cool completely in their liquid, then cover and refrigerate up to 1 week or freeze in their liquid up to 3 months.

Kale Pesto

Spicy and sweet kale leaves make a bright alternative to basil in pesto. Young kale with tender leaves is best for this recipe.

MAKES 2½ TO 3 CUPS

2 bunches green kale
1 garlic clove
1 teaspoon kosher salt
1 cup olive oil
½ cup finely grated Parmesan cheese

Strip the kale leaves from the stems and coarsely chop. Wash in cold water and drain. Peel the garlic clove. Add the kale leaves, garlic, salt, and ½ cup water to a blender and purée until smooth. Transfer the purée to a small bowl and stir in the olive oil and Parmesan. Taste for seasoning and adjust as needed.

VARIATION:
↬ Substitute parsley, rocket, or basil for the kale leaves.

Garlic Toasts

MAKES 10 TO 12 TOASTS

1 loaf whole wheat country-style bread
    (12 ounces)
3 tablespoons olive oil
2 garlic cloves

Preheat the oven to 450°F. Cut the bread into ¾-inch-thick slices and then cut each slice in half. Put the bread slices on a baking tray and brush with olive oil. Toast in the oven for 6 to 7 minutes. Rub a raw garlic clove on the surface of the toasts while still warm from the oven.

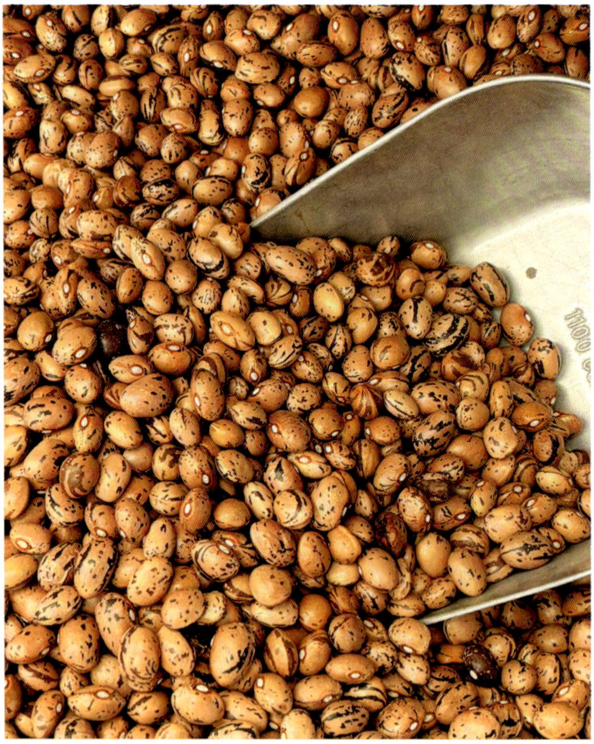

Cranberry Bean and Pasta Soup

This is the classic, simple, satisfying, much-loved Italian soup pasta e fagioli. Speckled cranberry (or borlotti) beans cooked until tender and creamy form the base of the soup. Pasta is added to blend with the beans and soak up the rich flavor.

MAKES 3 QUARTS

2 cups dried cranberry beans (1 pound)
3 bay leaves
1½ tablespoons kosher salt
1 large onion
1 celery stalk, trimmed

½ cup olive oil
16 ounces canned whole tomatoes
1 pound dried pasta (preferably small tubes such as tubetti or ditalini)

Put the beans in a large bowl, cover with 3 quarts cold water, and place in the refrigerator to soak overnight.

When you are ready to cook the beans, drain them and pour them into a pot. Add the bay leaves and salt and cover with 3½ quarts cold water. Cook over high heat until they come to a boil, then reduce the heat to a gentle simmer. Skim the foam that rises to the surface of the water, and continue cooking for 30 to 60 minutes, stirring occasionally, until the beans are tender but still a bit firm.

Peel and finely dice the onion and dice the celery. Heat a large heavy-bottomed pot over medium and add ½ cup olive oil and the diced onion and celery. Cook gently until the vegetables are soft and translucent, about 10 minutes. Chop the tomatoes or pass them through a food mill, add to the pot, and simmer for 5 to 10 minutes to soften.

Remove the aromatic vegetables and bay leaves from the beans, strain the beans and retain the broth. Add the beans to the pot with the tomatoes and stir. Add 2½ quarts of the bean broth and simmer the soup until the beans are completely tender, 10 to 15 minutes. Remove 2 to 3 cups of beans and broth from the pan and purée in a food processor or with an immersion blender, or pass through a food mill, and return to the pot. Taste for salt and adjust as needed.

Bring the soup to a boil and add the pasta. Cook, stirring frequently, until the pasta is tender, 8 to 10 minutes depending on the type of pasta. Have ready a small pan of boiling bean broth or water to add to the soup if it becomes too thick. Taste again for salt, adjust if needed, and serve hot with a drizzle of olive oil.

VARIATION:
↪ Use 2 cups chopped ripe tomatoes in place of canned.

Leek and Potato Soup

MAKES 2½ QUARTS

½ yellow onion
2 leeks
2 celery stalks, trimmed
2 garlic cloves
2 large russet potatoes
2 tablespoons olive oil
2 tablespoons kosher salt

Peel and thinly slice the onion. Cut off the root end and the green tops of the leeks and remove the tough outer layer. Cut the leeks in half lengthwise and rinse well under cold water. Thinly slice the leeks and celery. Peel and slice the garlic. Peel the potatoes and dice into ½-inch cubes. Set half of the potatoes aside in a bowl filled with cold water.

Heat the olive oil in a soup pot and add the onion, leeks, celery, and garlic. Cook the vegetables gently over medium-low heat until soft. Add half the potatoes, 2 quarts cold water, and the salt. Bring to a boil and then reduce the heat to a simmer. Cook, stirring occasionally, until the potatoes are soft, about 10 minutes. Use a spoon to smash a potato cube against the side of the pot to test if it is tender.

Purée the soup in batches in a blender and then return to the pot. (Be careful not to fill the blender more than halfway, use a towel to cover the lid, and make sure the lid is vented to allow the steam to escape.) Add the remaining potatoes and simmer the soup until the potatoes are cooked through. Taste for seasoning and adjust as needed.

Green Lentil Soup

Green lentils keep their shape when cooked, making a soup with lots of flavor and a chewy texture that doesn't turn into a purée like dal and other kinds of lentils. They are also great for salad with diced crunchy vegetables, spices, and herbs.

MAKES 2½ QUARTS

1 yellow onion, peeled
1 celery stalk, trimmed
3 carrots
2 garlic cloves
½ cup fresh cilantro leaves
3 tablespoons olive oil
2 bay leaves

1 tablespoon ground cumin
1 teaspoon ground coriander
2 cups French green lentils
2 tablespoons kosher salt
1 cup plain yogurt
1 cup fresh Italian parsley leaves

Finely dice the onion and celery. Peel the carrots and slice them into coins. Peel and mince the garlic and chop the cilantro. Put the vegetables, garlic, and cilantro in a soup pot and add the olive oil, bay leaves, and spices. Cook over medium heat for 10 minutes, or until softened.

Add the lentils, salt, and 3½ quarts cold water. Bring the soup to a gentle simmer and cook, stirring occasionally, until the lentils are tender all the way through, about 30 minutes. Remove the bay leaves, taste for seasoning, and add more salt if needed.

Place the yogurt in a small bowl. Chop the parsley and mix it into the yogurt with a pinch of salt. Garnish each bowl of soup with a spoonful of yogurt.

Pozole

Pozole is a traditional Mexican soup made with hominy (cooked dried corn kernels) and a full-flavored broth with tomatoes, sweet chiles, and cumin.

MAKES 4 QUARTS

1 skinless chicken breast fillet (½ pound)
1 tablespoon plus 1 teaspoon kosher salt
½ yellow onion, peeled
2 garlic cloves, peeled
2 tablespoons olive oil
1 bay leaf
3 dried guajillo chiles, seeded
1 tablespoon paprika
1 teaspoon ground cumin
1 teaspoon ground coriander
½ cup tomato purée
2 large carrots, peeled
1 celery stalk, trimmed
3 cups cooked hominy
5 corn tortillas
1½ cups vegetable oil
½ head green cabbage
1 bunch red radishes

Bring 1½ quarts water and 1 tablespoon salt to a boil and add the chicken breast. Reduce the heat to a gentle simmer and poach the chicken for 15 to 20 minutes, or until cooked through. Reserving the poaching broth, remove the chicken from the pot and let cool completely.

Dice the onion and mince the garlic. Put in a soup pot with the olive oil, 1 teaspoon salt, bay leaf, guajillo chiles, paprika, cumin, coriander, and 1 cup water. Cook over medium-low heat until the onion is completely tender, about 10 to 15 minutes. Add the tomato purée and the chicken poaching broth. Bring to a simmer and cook for 30 minutes, stirring occasionally. While the soup base cooks, dice the carrots and celery and shred the poached chicken into bite-size pieces.

Remove the bay leaf and purée the soup base in batches in a blender. (Be careful not to fill the blender more than halfway, use a towel to cover the lid, and make sure the lid is vented to allow the steam to escape.) Return the soup to the pot and add 1½ quarts water, the diced carrots and celery, and the hominy. Simmer until the carrots and celery are tender. Taste for salt and adjust if needed.

For the garnish: Slice the corn tortillas into ¼-inch strips. Heat a large cast-iron skillet over medium heat, add the vegetable oil, and heat it to frying temperature (375°F). Test with one tortilla strip—it should sizzle and start frying immediately;

if not, wait until it starts to fry. Add all the tortilla strips and stir constantly with a slotted spoon until they are golden brown and crispy. Remove to a baking sheet lined with paper towels to absorb excess oil, and allow to cool.

Remove the outer leaves and core from the cabbage and finely cut crosswise. Trim the tops and roots from the radishes and thinly slice.

Just before serving, add the chicken to the hot soup. Serve with the fried tortilla strips, cabbage, and radish slices on the side for each person to add to the soup as they like.

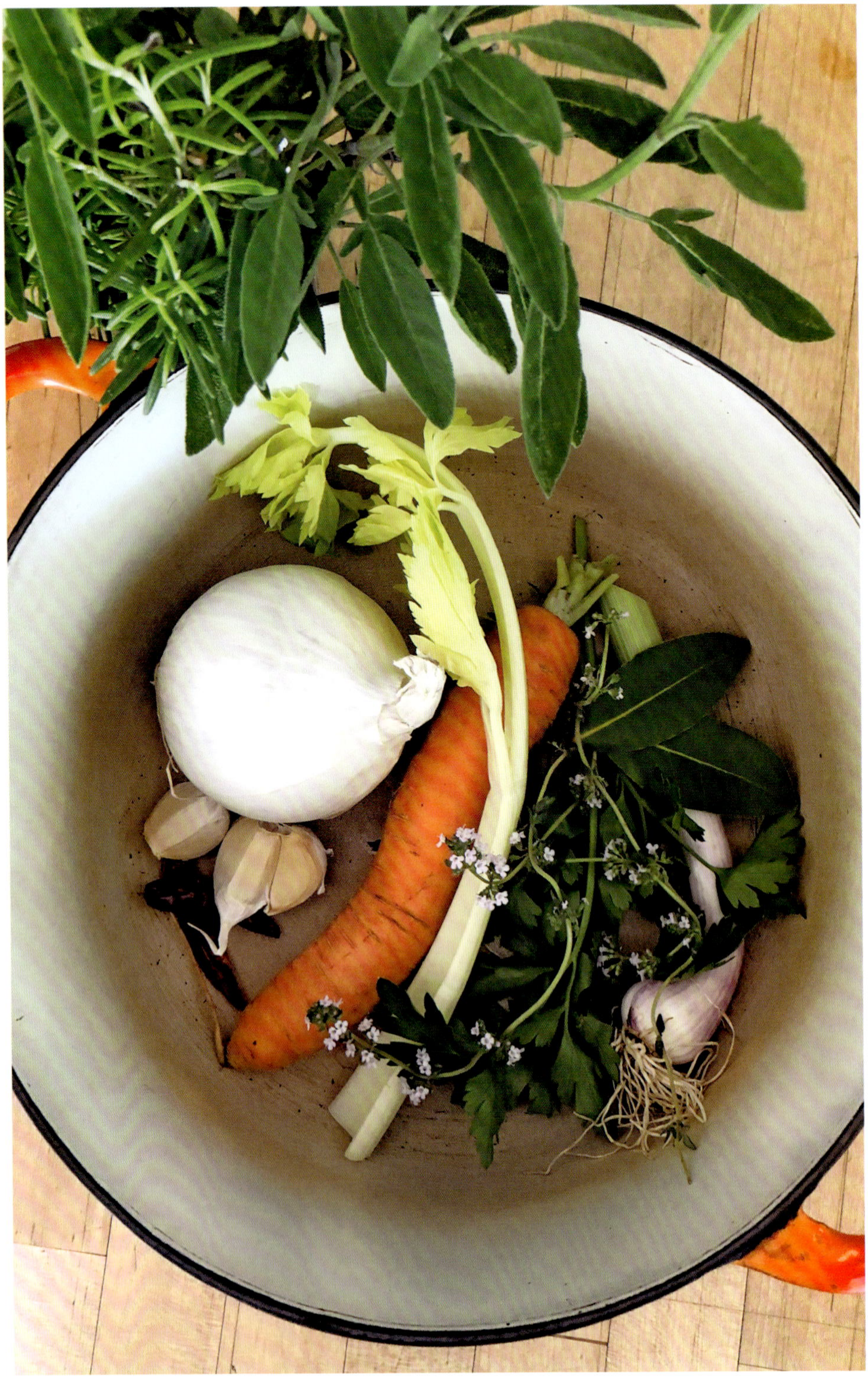

Meats and Stews

Meats are not only costly but also not as healthy overall as a plant-based diet. These recipes use moderate amounts of economical cuts of meat and poultry, flavored with spices, herbs, and chiles, and combined with vegetables and grains for tasty and balanced dishes.

Stews and braises fall into the category of good time management. Steps in the process can stretch over several days: preparing and seasoning the meat; slow cooking; finishing the sauce (removing any chilled fat); and preparing the servings. The flavors of a braise, such as the pork in Chile Braised Pork Tacos, always improve by resting a day. A quick stew of Chicken Tomato Curry doesn't require days of preparation and is delicious with Chickpeas and Brown Rice to soak up the sauce.

Barbecue Chicken Legs

Chicken drumsticks or whole legs are ideal for many cooking methods. They are delicious, tender, and fun to eat with your hands. In this recipe they are marinated in homemade barbecue sauce and roasted in the oven.

MAKES 10 DRUMSTICKS

10 chicken drumsticks
Kosher salt
1½ cups Barbecue Sauce (page 93)

Preheat the oven to 400°F.

Season each chicken leg evenly and lightly with salt, about ½ teaspoon per leg. This may vary with the size of the chicken legs.

Put the chicken in a bowl, toss with the barbecue sauce, and let marinate for 20 to 30 minutes. Put the legs in a shallow half hotel pan and place in the oven. Roast for 20 minutes, then turn the legs over and continue roasting another 30 to 40 minutes, or until browned and the internal temperature reads 165°F.

VARIATION:
- Marinate the chicken with other flavor combinations such as a mixture of pounded garlic, lemon zest and juice, and herbs, or a dry rub of spices with cardamom, black pepper, and coriander.

Barbecue Sauce

Barbecue sauce can be used in many ways—as a marinade for meats, a dipping sauce, or a condiment. It is smoky, tangy, and sweet and surprisingly simple to make.

MAKES 3 CUPS

½ onion
1 garlic clove
2 teaspoons kosher salt
¼ cup olive oil
2 cups water
1 tablespoon smoked paprika
1 tablespoon sweet paprika

1 teaspoon dry mustard
1 teaspoon ground cumin
¼ cup cider vinegar
2 tablespoons molasses
1 tablespoon honey
¾ cup tomato paste

Peel and dice the onion and peel and mince the garlic. Add to a saucepan with the salt, olive oil, and ½ cup water. Simmer until the water has evaporated and the onion is soft and translucent, about 10 minutes.

Stir in 1½ cups water and all the remaining ingredients, and continue to gently simmer for 25 to 30 minutes. Transfer the sauce to a blender and purée. (Be careful not to fill the blender more than halfway, use a towel to cover the lid, and make sure the lid is vented to allow the steam to escape.) It should be the consistency of a thick puréed soup. If it is a little thin, return to the pot and reduce, stirring often, until it thickens. Allow to cool completely.

Meatballs and Tomato Sauce

MAKES THIRTY 1¼-INCH MEATBALLS

1 pound ground pork
2 teaspoons kosher salt
¼ teaspoon fresh-ground black pepper
1 cup torn pieces day-old country-style bread, crusts removed
½ cup milk
1 small onion
1 garlic clove

2 tablespoons chopped fresh parsley leaves
1 tablespoon chopped fresh marjoram or oregano leaves
1 tablespoon olive oil
1 egg
1½ quarts Tomato Sauce (page 42)
Polenta (page 47; optional)

Put the pork in a bowl and season with the salt and pepper. Combine the bread and milk in a small bowl and set aside to soften. Preheat the oven to 400°F.

Peel the onion and grate using the large holes of a box grater. Peel the garlic clove and pound to a paste in a small mortar with a pinch of salt. Add the onion, garlic, parsley, marjoram, and olive oil to the meat. Squeeze most of the milk out of the bread and add the bread to the meat mixture along with the egg.

Combine the ingredients with your hands, gently but thoroughly, or put them in the bowl of a stand mixer and mix on low speed with the paddle attachment for 2 to 3 minutes. Use a small ice cream scoop or a spoon to form the mixture into 1¼-inch balls. Place them on a rimmed baking sheet lined with parchment paper. Bake the meatballs until cooked through, about 20 minutes. Turn the pan midway through for even browning.

When ready to serve, heat the tomato sauce, add the meatballs, and bring to a simmer. If you like, spoon the meatballs and sauce over warm Polenta (page 47).

VARIATIONS:
- Use a combination of turkey or chicken and pork, or beef and pork, or all beef instead of pork.
- Add other chopped fresh herbs such as cilantro, mint, sage, or thyme, in whatever combination you like.
- Add ¼ cup grated Parmesan or pecorino cheese to the mixture.
- Substitute cold cooked rice or potato for the soaked bread.
- Serve topped with grated Parmesan or pecorino cheese.

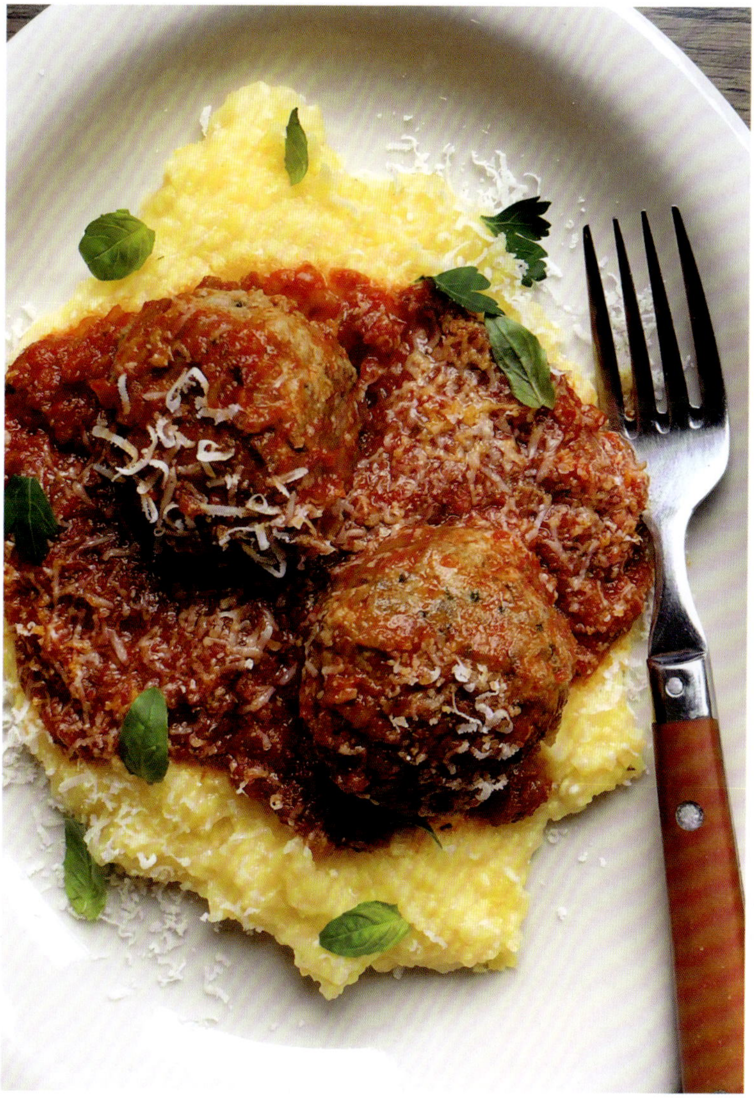

Spicy Lamb Meatballs

These meatballs are made with the aromatic spices typical of North Africa and are delicious served with the fluffy pasta-like Couscous (page 71) of the region.

MAKES THIRTY 1¼-INCH MEATBALLS

1 cup fresh whole wheat breadcrumbs	½ yellow onion, peeled and grated
½ cup milk	1 garlic clove, peeled and pounded to a paste
1 pound ground lamb	1 tablespoon chopped fresh cilantro leaves
2 teaspoons kosher salt	
¼ teaspoon fresh-ground black pepper	1 egg, lightly beaten
	½ tablespoon olive oil
1 tablespoon ground cumin	1 recipe Spicy Meatball Sauce (page 97)
1 teaspoon ground coriander	
1 teaspoon ground fennel	Couscous (page 71)

Preheat the oven to 400°F.

Mix the breadcrumbs and milk in a small bowl and let sit for 10 to 15 minutes. Squeeze the excess milk from the breadcrumbs and put them in a large mixing bowl with the remaining ingredients, except the olive oil and meatball sauce, and use your hands to mix gently but thoroughly. Alternatively, combine the ingredients in the bowl of a stand mixer and mix on low speed with the paddle attachment for 2 to 3 minutes.

Use a small ice cream scoop or a spoon to form the mixture into 1¼-inch balls. Place on a rimmed baking sheet lined with parchment paper and drizzle lightly with the olive oil. Bake for 25 minutes, turning the pan once or twice for even cooking. Reheat the meatballs in the sauce and serve with couscous.

VARIATIONS:
- Use other ground meats, singly or in combination, in place of the lamb.
- Vary the spices to taste or replace them with lots of chopped fresh herbs.

Spicy Meatball Sauce

MAKES 1¾ QUARTS

½ large yellow onion, peeled
5 garlic cloves, peeled
½ cup fresh cilantro leaves
2 tablespoons olive oil
1 teaspoon ground cumin
1 teaspoon ground coriander
¼ teaspoon cinnamon
2 (28-ounce) cans tomato purée
  (7 cups or 1¾ quarts)
2 teaspoons kosher salt

Finely dice the onion. Mince the garlic and chop the cilantro. Heat a saucepan over medium heat and add the olive oil, onion, garlic, cilantro, and spices. Cook gently, stirring often, until the onion is completely soft, about 10 to 15 minutes. Add the tomato purée and salt and simmer for 10 minutes. Taste and adjust the seasoning if needed.

Chile Braised Pork Tacos

This is a very tasty, versatile pork braise—easy, economical, and crowd-pleasing. The meat is cooked until quite tender and can be kept warm and served straightaway or chilled in its sauce and served another day. The meat in its juices freezes very well and is good to have on hand to add to beans, pasta, or vegetables for a satisfying meal. It is great shredded and warmed in its juices for tacos served with Tomato Salsa (page 99) and Napa Cabbage Slaw (page 30). It is also delicious with Polenta (page 47), with beans and sautéed greens, or with mashed potatoes.

MAKES 10 SERVINGS (20 SMALL TACOS)

One 3- to 4-pound, bone-in pork shoulder roast
1 tablespoon kosher salt
¼ teaspoon fresh-ground black pepper
1 tablespoon chopped fresh marjoram or oregano
1 teaspoon ground ancho chile
2 onions
2 carrots
1 large head garlic
3 dried ancho chiles
1 dried chipotle chile
A few black peppercorns
40 small, thin corn tortillas
Tomato Salsa (page 99)
20 small radishes, trimmed and quartered
3 limes, quartered
Napa Cabbage Slaw (page 30)

Trim the roast of excess fat. Make a dry rub by mixing the salt, pepper, 1 tablespoon chopped marjoram, and ground ancho chile. Use the dry rub to season the roast (the day before, if possible). Cover and refrigerate until 1 hour before cooking.

Preheat the oven to 375°F. Peel and coarsely chop the onions, carrots, and garlic. Split the dried chiles in half and remove the seeds. Put the onions, carrots, garlic, ancho and chipotle chiles, peppercorns, and marjoram sprigs in a heavy baking dish or roasting pan that just fits the roast, place the seasoned meat on top of the vegetables, and pour in 2 cups water. The water should reach about one-quarter of the way up the roast. Add more if needed.

Cook the roast in the oven for 1 hour and 15 minutes. Check the level of the liquid every once in a while, adding more water as needed to maintain a consistent level. Turn the roast over and cook for 30 more minutes, then turn again and cook for 30 more minutes. Test the meat for doneness, continuing to turn and cook as needed until very tender.

Remove the meat from the pan. Strain the sauce and skim well. Remove the bone, shred or slice the meat, remove excess fat, and keep warm, moistened with the juices.

To serve the tacos, arrange 10 plates with 2 pairs of warm tortillas each and top each pair with shredded pork and salsa. Garnish the plate with quartered radishes, lime wedges, and Napa Cabbage Slaw (page 30).

VARIATIONS:
- Serve with avocado salsa in place of tomato salsa, or add slices of avocado to the tacos.
- In place of salsa, top the pork with spicy cabbage slaw.
- Cook a 3- to 4-pound boneless pork roast in place of a bone-in cut.
- In place of or in addition to the pork, make tacos with warm beans topped with toasted cumin seeds and cheese.

Tomato Salsa

MAKES 2 CUPS

4 medium ripe tomatoes or 8 canned whole tomatoes
2 garlic cloves, peeled and finely chopped

1 red or white onion, peeled and diced
½ bunch cilantro, chopped
Juice of 1 lime
Kosher salt

Core and dice the tomatoes. Combine in a bowl with the remaining ingredients and salt to taste. Stir gently, taste, and add more lime juice and salt as needed. Let sit 5 minutes for the flavors to develop.

VARIATIONS:
- For a spicy salsa, add 2 finely chopped jalapeño or serrano chiles.
- Add ½ teaspoon crushed toasted cumin seeds.
- Fold in 1 avocado cut into medium dice.

Chicken Tomato Curry

This is a savory chicken stew rich with aromatic spices. It is delicious served with warm chickpeas and rice to soak up the flavorful sauce.
MAKES 8 TO 10 SERVINGS

10 chicken drumsticks or 5 thighs
3 tablespoons kosher salt
1 yellow onion
2-inch piece ginger
4 garlic cloves
2 tablespoons cumin seeds
1 tablespoon coriander seeds
1 teaspoon fennel seeds
3 or 4 whole cloves
½ teaspoon ground cinnamon
½ teaspoon ground turmeric
4 tablespoons olive oil
1 bay leaf
2 cups tomato purée
½ cup sour cream
Chickpeas and Brown Rice (page 101)

Season the chicken evenly with 2 tablespoons salt and let sit for 30 minutes (or up to 1 day in advance, refrigerated). Peel and dice the onion. Peel and mince the ginger and garlic. Put the cumin, coriander, and fennel seeds and cloves in a spice grinder and grind to a fine powder. Mix in the cinnamon and turmeric.

Heat a medium-size, heavy-bottomed pot and add 2 tablespoons olive oil. When the oil is hot, add the chicken legs and cook for 10 to 15 minutes, until evenly browned on all sides. Remove the chicken from the pot. Add the remaining 2 tablespoons olive oil, onion, ginger, garlic, and bay leaf. Cook gently for about 10 minutes, until the onion has softened. Add the spices and cook for 1 to 2 minutes to toast them. Add the tomato purée and 1 cup water and simmer for 10 to 15 minutes.

Remove the bay leaf and blend the sauce in a blender or food processor until smooth. Add back to the pot with 2 cups water and the remaining 1 tablespoon salt. Add the chicken legs and simmer over low heat until the meat is tender and starting to fall off the bone, about 45 minutes. Remove the legs from the sauce and let cool. When cool enough to handle, shred the meat from the bones and return it to the sauce. Simmer for a few minutes to heat thoroughly, then stir in the sour cream to finish the sauce.

Serve with Chickpeas and Brown Rice.

Chickpeas and Brown Rice

MAKES 10 SERVINGS (1½ QUARTS)

2 cups brown rice
1 teaspoon kosher salt

2 cups cooked chickpeas (page 62)
1 teaspoon ground turmeric

Put the rice, 4 cups water, and salt in a pot and bring to a boil. Cover with a tight-fitting lid and reduce the heat to a simmer. Cook for 40 to 45 minutes, until the rice is tender and cooked through. Turn off the heat and let rest, still covered, for another 10 minutes. Fluff with a fork before serving.

Heat the chickpeas in a pot with some of their cooking liquid or a little water. Add the turmeric and simmer for a few minutes to heat through. Strain the chickpeas (save the cooking liquid for another use), stir into the rice, and serve.

VARIATION:
- If you like, add some of the strained chickpea-turmeric cooking liquid to the Chicken Tomato Curry sauce to make it looser and thinner.

Red Bean Chili

This chili is made with tasty small red beans and turkey. If you like, use other meats in place of turkey or make a vegetarian version, but Cornbread (page 46) alongside is a must!

MAKES 4 QUARTS

1 carrot, peeled
1 celery stalk, trimmed
½ onion, peeled
½ fennel bulb
2 garlic cloves
2 tablespoons olive oil
1 bay leaf
½ teaspoon smoked paprika

1 teaspoon ground cumin
1 cup farro or barley
3 tablespoons kosher salt
1 pound ground turkey
1½ cups tomato purée
3 cups Red Beans (page 103)
Cornbread (page 46)

Finely dice the carrot, celery, onion, and fennel. Peel and mince the garlic.

Heat the olive oil in a large pot and add the diced vegetables, garlic, bay leaf, paprika, cumin, farro, and 1½ tablespoons salt. Cook over medium-low heat for 15 to 20 minutes, stirring often, until all the vegetables are soft but not browned.

Add the ground turkey, tomato purée, and remaining salt to the pot and bring to a simmer. Stir well to break apart the turkey. Add 5 cups cold water and return to a simmer. Stirring occasionally, cook the chili for 1 hour, or until the turkey is tender and the liquid has thickened slightly. Gently stir in the cooked beans so they don't break apart and simmer for another 10 minutes. Add some of the bean broth if the chili needs more liquid. Taste for seasoning and adjust if needed. Serve hot with fresh cornbread.

VARIATIONS:

- Use red kidney beans or a mixture of several different types of beans in place of the red beans.
- Add chopped kale or other hearty greens. In the summertime, add fresh corn kernels and diced red bell peppers.
- For a vegetarian version, cook the chili without turkey and double the quantity of beans.

Red Beans

MAKES 1¾ QUARTS

2½ cups dried red beans (1¼ pounds)	½ onion, peeled
	1 head garlic, cut in half
½ carrot, peeled	1 bay leaf
½ celery stalk	1½ tablespoons kosher salt

Put the beans in a large bowl, cover with 3 quarts cold water, and place in the refrigerator to soak overnight.

When you are ready to cook the beans, drain them and pour them into a pot. Add the carrot, celery, onion, garlic, bay leaf, and salt and cover with 3 quarts cold water. Bring to a boil over high heat, then reduce the heat to a gentle simmer. Skim the foam that rises to the surface of the water, and continue cooking for 1 to 2 hours, stirring occasionally, until the beans are completely tender. Discard aromatic vegetables and bay leaf.

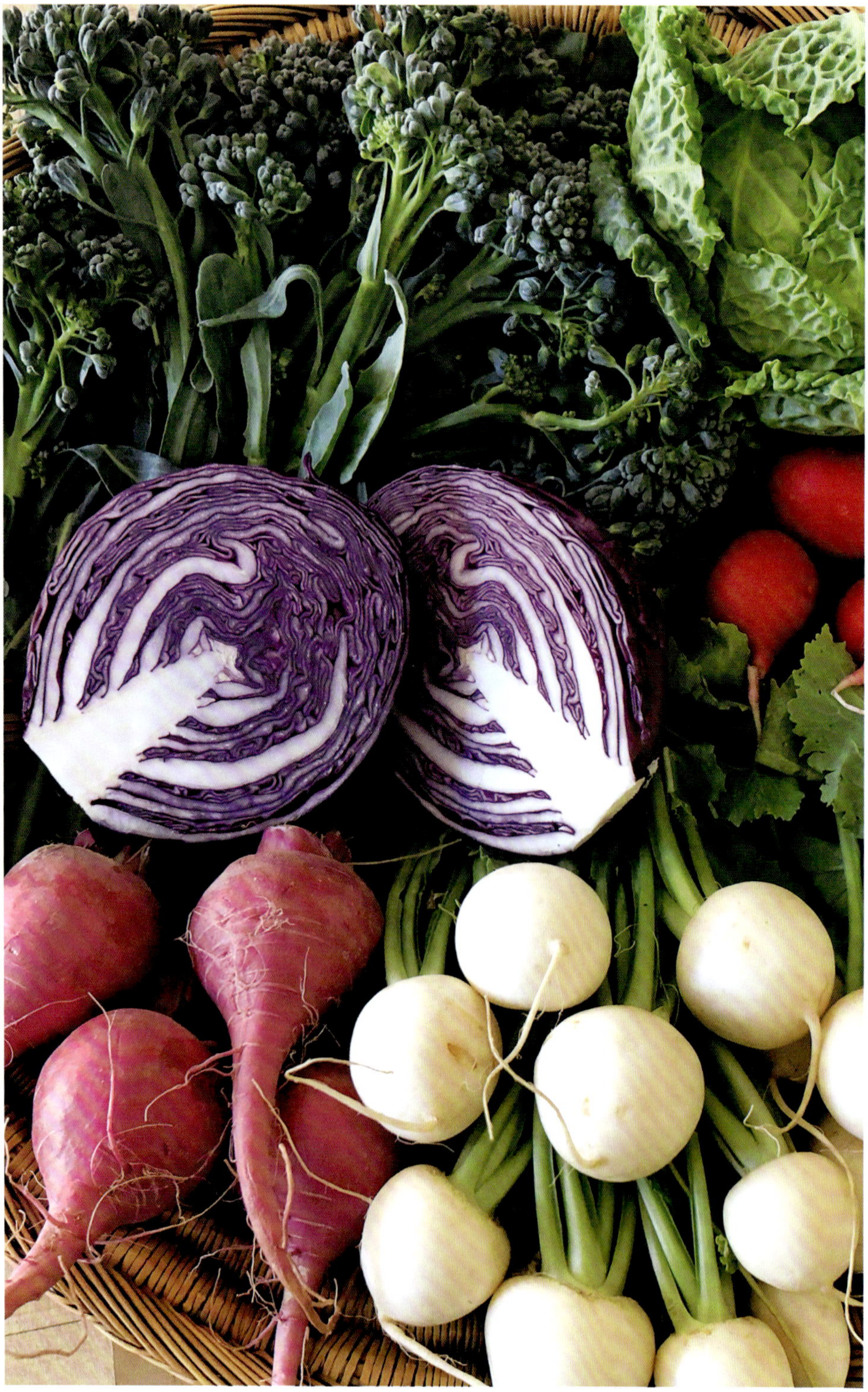

Vegetables

The school year begins again each year in August and September, when summer produce is at its peak in flavor and supply—tomatoes of all colors and sizes, sweet and bicolor corn, spicy and sweet peppers, summer squashes and squash blossoms, green and yellow beans and shell beans, potatoes, avocados, cucumbers, herbs, garlic, stone fruits, berries. Menu options abound: tomato salads, soups, sauces, and salsas; corn on the cob, sautéed corn, corn soup; peppers for dipping and for salads; summer squash in quesadillas, with pasta and pesto, roasted, and skewered; avocados and cucumbers for salads and salsas; herbs and garlic for pesto, chimichurri, and other sauces and salads.

As the weather and light change, summer crops give way to fall and winter vegetables. The cooler temperatures favor cabbages, leafy greens, chicories, and lettuces, and the first of the winter squashes and root vegetables sweetened by cold temperatures arrive: butternut, delicata, acorn, and dumpling squashes, carrots, parsnips, rutabagas, celery root, and kohlrabi.

Spring starts slowly with leeks, fava beans, snap peas and English peas, crisp spinach, new carrots and fennel, green garlic, scarlet and Tokyo turnips, cauliflower, tender lettuces, and rocket. Early summer follows soon with broccolini, cucumbers, squash blossoms, the first Romano beans, cherry tomatoes, and new potatoes.

A few methods of preparation serve well through all the seasons. Many vegetables in many combinations, some raw and some simply blanched, can be tossed with lively dressings and made into fresh salads. Quick-cooking vegetables, such as corn and tender greens, are good lightly sautéed. Roasting vegetables is one of the easiest cooking methods, and the results are amazingly good. Leafy greens are delicious blanched until tender and then flavored with garlic and spices. Collards and sturdy greens develop savory flavors through slow, long cooking.

Sautéed Corn with Chile and Lime

Sautéed sweet corn is an alternative to boiling corn on the cob and an opportunity to flavor the corn directly with the complementary flavors of chile and lime.
MAKES 8 SERVINGS

10 ears corn
1 yellow onion, or 2 small red onions
2 jalapeño or serrano chiles
½ bunch cilantro

½ cup butter or vegetable oil
Kosher salt
Juice of 1 or 2 limes

Shuck the corn and use a towel to rub away the silk. Cut the kernels off the cob and set aside. (To cut the kernels from the cob, hold on to the stem end, pointing the tip of the ear down, and run your knife down the cob.) Peel and dice the onion fine. Cut the chiles in half, remove the seeds (if you like more heat, leave them), and dice fine. Pick the cilantro leaves from the stems and chop fine.

Melt the butter in a heavy skillet over medium heat. Add the onion and chiles and cook for 3 to 4 minutes to soften. Turn up the heat to medium-high and add the corn. Sauté for a few minutes, stirring, until the corn is cooked; if needed, moisten with a splash of water. Season to taste with salt and lime juice, add the chopped cilantro, and serve.

VARIATIONS:
- Use frozen corn in place of fresh corn.
- Omit the chiles and cilantro, sauté the corn and onion in butter, and season to taste.
- Substitute basil for the cilantro.
- In place of green chiles, add diced sweet red peppers.

Baby Bok Choy and Tamari Sauce

Sweet and mild baby bok choy (pak choi), with dark green leaves and crisp white ribs, cooks very quickly. Keep a close eye so that it doesn't cook past tender and lose its crisp texture. Chinese broccoli is delicious cooked this way as well.

MAKES 8 TO 10 SERVINGS

FOR THE TAMARI SAUCE:
- ¾ cup tamari
- 3 tablespoons rice vinegar
- 1 tablespoon freshly grated ginger or garlic
- 2 teaspoons sesame oil
- ½ teaspoon sugar or honey

FOR THE BOK CHOY:
- 10 baby bok choy (or equivalent larger bok choy halved or quartered)
- 1 tablespoon vegetable oil or coconut oil
- 6 garlic cloves, smashed
- 3 slices ginger, peeled and smashed
- Kosher salt

Whisk the ingredients for the sauce together, taste for balance, and adjust as needed.

Remove and discard any damaged outer leaves from the bok choy. Wash well and drain.

Heat a heavy-bottomed pan over medium-high heat. Add the vegetable oil, garlic, and ginger and cook until the garlic just starts to color, then add the bok choy. Cook, stirring and tossing, until just tender, about 4 to 5 minutes. Season lightly with the salt. Serve with a small dish of tamari sauce.

Sweet Potato Wedges

Oven-roasted sweet potatoes are a popular, tasty, and healthy alternative to fried potatoes. Kids love them. They are delicious served with tangy Raita (page 40) for dipping. Some orange-fleshed varieties include Beauregard, garnet, jewel, and nugget. Depending on the variety and condition of the sweet potatoes, peel them or not, as you like.

MAKES 8 SERVINGS

3 pounds sweet potatoes
Olive oil or vegetable oil
Kosher salt and fresh-ground black pepper

Preheat the oven to 400°F.

Wash and scrub the sweet potatoes if leaving the skins on, or peel to remove the skins. Cut the sweet potatoes into wedges or half-moon slices ⅓ to ½ inch thick. Put them in a bowl, drizzle with the olive oil, season with the salt and pepper, and toss to coat evenly. Spread them out on a baking sheet lined with parchment paper and bake until tender and lightly browned, 25 to 30 minutes.

VARIATIONS:
- Toss the sweet potatoes with leaves of fresh thyme, rosemary, marjoram, or sage along with the oil and salt.
- Along with the oil and salt, toss with ½ teaspoon cumin seeds lightly crushed in a mortar, or if you like, freshly grated orange zest.

Mashed Potatoes and Celery Root

Celery root has a mild flavor that combines beautifully with potato and makes an ordinary mash into something special. These proportions are half and half, but more or less of either vegetable is fine, or just potatoes alone.

MAKES 8 SERVINGS

2 medium celery roots (about 1½ pounds)
Kosher salt

2 pounds Yukon Gold or other yellow-fleshed potatoes
6 tablespoons butter
Milk, as needed (optional)

Peel and trim the roots from the celery roots. Cut into ½-inch slices and then into medium dice. Boil in salted water until soft, about 10 minutes. Remove the celery roots, reserving the water.

Peel and cut the potatoes into large dice. Cook in boiling salted water used to cook the celery root, or use another pot of salted water. Drain.

Pass the vegetables through a ricer or food mill and return to the pot. Gently reheat and stir in the butter. Taste for seasoning and add salt as needed. If the mash is too thick, thin with a little milk.

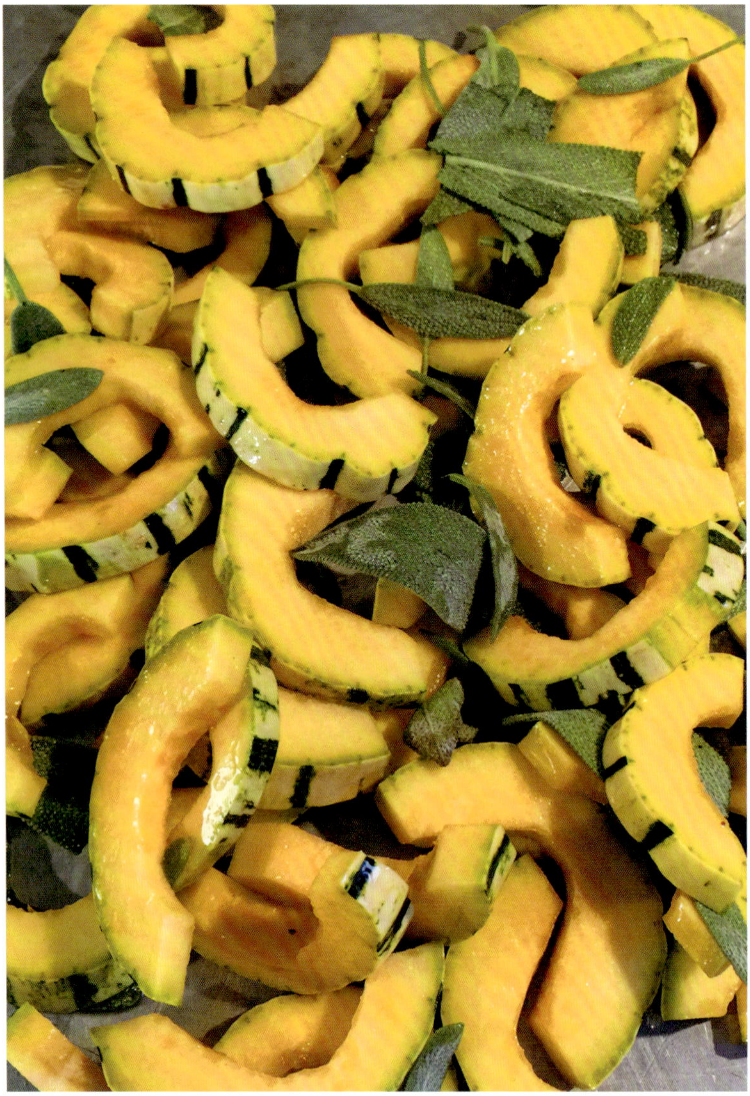

Roasted Delicata Squash

Thin-skinned delicata squash is especially delicious roasted. Its natural sugars caramelize in the oven, intensifying the flavor and aroma. The same method works for many other vegetables: carrots, rutabagas, celery root, turnips, parsnips, kohlrabi, potatoes, broccoli, sweet potatoes, cauliflower, eggplant, fennel.

Cut the vegetables into pieces more or less the same size for even cooking, and with an eye to beautiful shapes. Roast in a hot oven, preheated to 400°F; the vegetables can dry out if cooked at lower temperatures. Cooking times will vary with different vegetables; cook until tender and nicely browned but not too dark.

MAKES 10 SERVINGS

5 small delicata squash
2 tablespoons olive oil or vegetable oil
Kosher salt

Preheat the oven to 400°F.

There is no need to peel the colorful thin skin of the squash; it is tender when cooked. Wash the squash, cut in half lengthwise, and scoop out the seeds. Cut the squash crosswise into ½-inch-thick slices. Place the slices in a bowl and toss with the olive oil and lightly salt. Spread on a baking sheet lined with parchment paper and roast until tender and caramelized, about 20 minutes.

VARIATIONS:
- Toss with chopped fresh marjoram, sage, or thyme leaves before roasting.
- In place of delicata, roast other winter squashes, peeled if thick-skinned, either sliced or diced.

Sautéed Greens

This is a reliable and simple method of cooking various kinds of leafy greens. Stem the greens and, depending on their size and final use, stack the leaves and cut into smaller pieces or leave them in larger strips. The greens are delicious served with Cranberry Beans (page 58), Cannellini Beans (page 82), or other bean varieties.
MAKES 6 TO 8 SERVINGS

2 bunches chard
2 bunches kale
Kosher salt
2 tablespoons olive oil

1 large yellow onion, peeled and finely diced
4 garlic cloves, peeled and minced

Strip the chard leaves from the stems and wash well. Do the same with the kale. Blanch both types of greens separately in plenty of salted water until very tender, 3 to 4 minutes. Drain and let cool a bit. Roughly chop both and mix them together.

Heat a pot over medium heat, add the olive oil and onion, season lightly with salt, and cook until tender. Add the garlic and sizzle briefly without browning. Add the greens and mix thoroughly with the onion and garlic until heated through. Taste and add more salt as needed.

VARIATIONS:
- Add a pinch of dried red chile flakes to the onions if you like a bit of spice.
- Beet greens, turnip greens, young collard greens, and broccoli rabe are also delicious cooked this way.

Collard Greens

Collard greens develop deep, savory flavors and tenderness from long cooking to provide the perfect complement to black-eyed peas and other beans.
MAKES 8 SERVINGS

3 bunches collard greens
1 yellow onion
2 celery stalks, trimmed
3 garlic cloves
¼ cup olive oil

1 bay leaf
2 tablespoons kosher salt
1 cup tomato purée
1 teaspoon smoked paprika

Strip the collard leaves from the tough stems and coarsely chop the leaves. Wash in cold water and drain. Peel and cut the onion into ¼-inch dice. Thinly slice the celery crosswise. Peel and finely chop the garlic.

Heat a heavy-bottomed soup pot over medium heat and add the olive oil, onion, celery, garlic, bay leaf, salt, and 1 cup water. Cook, stirring occasionally, until the onion is soft, about 10 minutes. Add the tomato purée and paprika and cook for 5 minutes. Add the collard greens to the pot with 2 quarts water and bring to a boil. Reduce the heat to a simmer and cook the collards for 1 to 1½ hours, until very tender. Stir occasionally and monitor the water level; if the greens start to get dry, add small amounts of water as needed. Taste for seasoning and serve hot.

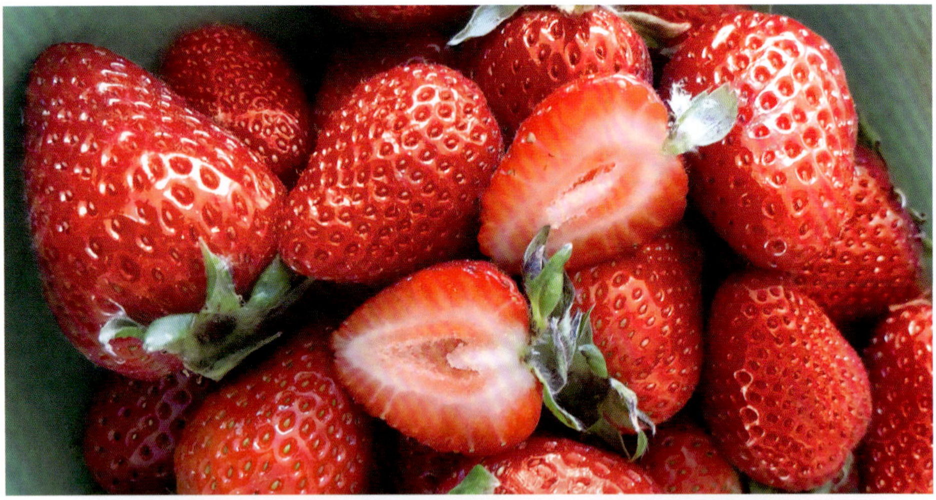
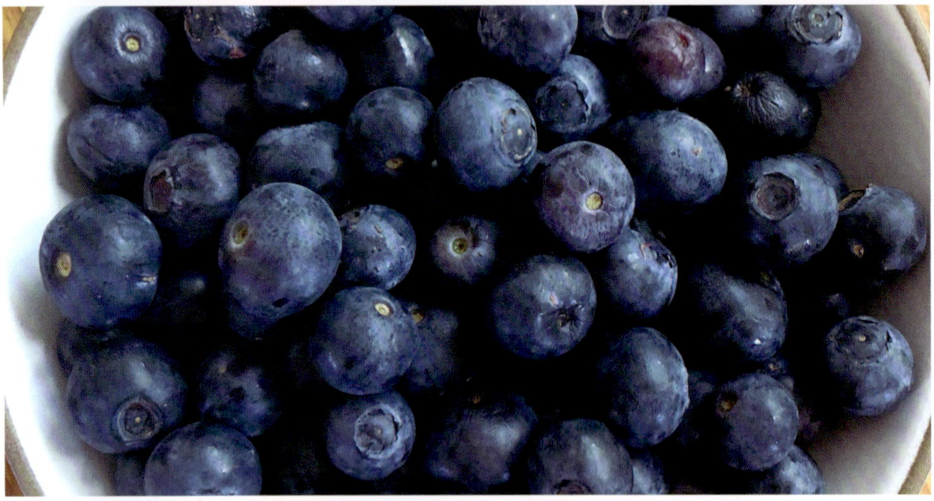
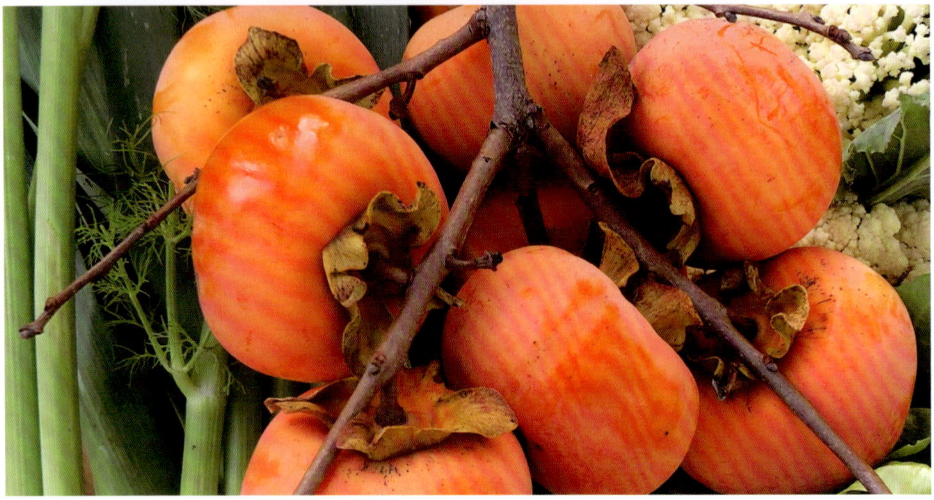

Fruits

Ripe fruit is a gift of nature, and fruits are an important and nutritious part of any diet. For me that's easy—I always prefer a piece of ripe fruit to a sweet dessert. It is especially important to include fresh fruit in children's meals and to feed them wholesome organic fruit instead of something sugary that they don't need.

Fragile summer fruits seem to come all at once, fleeting pleasures to be enjoyed ripe and raw: plums, pluots, white and yellow nectarines and peaches of many varieties, juicy melons, strawberries, blueberries, blackberries, boysenberries, and the like. Tender fruits, in almost any combination, make delicious compotes, either macerated and raw or cooked gently with a little syrup.

Local regional harvests of apples begin in late summer and early fall with a succession of varieties, each with their distinct virtues of flavor, texture, color, tartness, and cooking qualities.

There are literally thousands of delicious varieties adapted to regional climates and conditions, and they are a far cry from the ubiquitous and insipid Red Delicious. Crisp apples that are not too sweet, such as Sierra Beauty, Cox's Orange Pippin, and Granny Smith, are good for salads and cooking. Juicy, sweet Jonagold, Golden Delicious, and Pink Pearl make lovely applesauce and require little or no sugar.

Grapes and pears join the parade in early fall. Blushing, firm, and juicy Bartletts are always popular and reliable. Tender butter pear types are quite fragile and perishable but have superb flavor. Asian pears are crunchy like apples, with mild flavor. Graceful Bosc pears are excellent for poaching and baking.

Winter brings brilliant Fuyu persimmons, pomegranates, and new crops of mandarins, oranges, grapefruit, and other bright citrus fruits.

A whole raw apple or pear that is juicy and full of flavor needs no embellishment or preparation. Most kids love them, but for some a whole fruit is too much and can end up in the compost bin. When my daughter was young, I could always entice her to eat fruit if I cut it in slices or bite-size pieces—a simple bowl of sliced strawberries with bananas and orange juice, a cup of diced fruit, or slices of apple, pear, or persimmon added to a salad.

Fruit can be costly; the best prices are to be found when crops are at their peak and supply is greatest. Take advantage of excess fruits with a simple dehydrator and make your own excellent dried fruits. Overripe fruit can be made into fruit crisps, compotes, jams, and preserves.

Strawberry and Orange Bowl

A compote of strawberries and oranges can be as simple as sliced strawberries marinated in orange juice or a blend of sliced berries and sliced orange sections—any combination works. Orange juice sweetens the berries, so no sugar is needed.
MAKES 8 SERVINGS

3 pints ripe strawberries
2 or 3 oranges

Hull and slice the strawberries or cut into quarters. Juice the oranges and add to the bowl of berries. Mix together gently and let macerate for at least 30 minutes.

VARIATIONS:
- If you like, cut away the rind and pith of the oranges, cut into slices or segments, and add to the berries. Collect any juices and add to the fruits.
- Add sliced bananas to the bowl or substitute them for a third of the strawberries.
- Substitute other berries, such as blueberries, blackberries, or raspberries, for some of the strawberries. If extra sweetness is needed, add a bit of sugar or honey.

Summer Berry Compote

Berries are fragile and beautiful, and always loved by children. Make the most of them when they're abundant, in season, and most affordable.
MAKES 6 SERVINGS

1 pint strawberries
2 tablespoons sugar
1½ pints berries: blueberries, blackberries, raspberries, and boysenberries in any combination, depending on availability

Wash the strawberries, pat dry, and hull. Slice them into a bowl and toss with the sugar. Let them macerate for 15 minutes or so, until they release some juice. Add the rest of the berries and toss together gently. The longer they sit, the juicier they will be.

Fall Fruit Cup

I love the flavors and colors of fall fruits, the succession of apple and pear varieties, brilliant pomegranates, and crisp, bright orange Fuyu persimmons. They go together perfectly and make a beautiful fruit salad.
MAKES 8 SERVINGS

3 Bartlett pears
3 crisp tart apples
3 Fuyu persimmons
1 or 2 oranges
1 or 2 pomegranates

Wash, halve or quarter, and core the pears, apples, and persimmons. Cut them as you like into bite-size pieces or slices and combine in a bowl. Juice the oranges, pour the juice over the fruits, and toss gently. (The acidic orange juice will help keep the fruits from browning.) Remove the seeds from the pomegranates.

Serve soon after cutting and preparing the fruits, so they will be at their best. Spoon the fruit into bowls and sprinkle generously with the pomegranate seeds.

fruits

Applesauce

The best apples for applesauce and cooking are juicy with a bright balance of sweetness and tartness, such as Jonagold, Golden Delicious, McIntosh, beautiful rosy-fleshed Pink Pearl, Pink Lady, and many others. Many varieties require no added sugar. If you like, add a bit of cinnamon, but not so much that it overwhelms the apple flavor. Serve applesauce warm or at room temperature.

Six pounds of apples will yield about 3 cups of applesauce. Quarter and core the apples. Peel them or not, as you prefer. Cut the quarters into chunks. Put them in a saucepan and add apple juice or water to a depth of ½ inch. Simmer, covered, over medium heat, stirring occasionally, for 20 to 30 minutes, until the apples are cooked through, soft, and translucent. Add more juice or water as needed if the apples are a bit dry. Mash with a potato masher, or if you like a smooth applesauce, pass the apples through a food mill or food processor. Taste for sweetness and add a bit of sugar or lemon juice if needed.

Baked Apples

Any number of apples are delicious baked. Perhaps the best for baking are firm, not too sweet, not too big, not too small. Again, the fruits at peak season and locally available will be your best choice.

MAKES 8 SERVINGS

8 tart apples
½ cup sugar or brown sugar
Cinnamon and lemon zest (optional)
3 tablespoons butter, plus more for greasing
Heavy or whipped cream (optional)

Preheat the oven to 375°F.

Wash the apples, remove each core to ½ inch from the bottom, then cut a strip of peel from the bottom of each apple. Fill the center of each apple with 1 tablespoon sugar and flavor with cinnamon and lemon zest, if you like. Lightly butter a shallow baking dish large enough to hold all the apples and place them in the dish. Dot the top of each apple with about 1 teaspoon butter, cover them, and bake for 40 to 60 minutes, until tender but not mushy.

Remove from the oven and baste the apples several times with the juices. Serve warm or chilled, with or without poured or whipped cream.

VARIATION:
- Bake pears in a similar way: Peel Bosc pears, cut in half, and remove the cores. Arrange cut-side up in a baking dish. Sprinkle lightly with sugar and lemon zest, and put a dot of butter in each core cavity. Cover and bake as above, basting occasionally, until tender.

Baked Peaches

While eating fresh ripe peaches out of hand may be the best way to enjoy them, when you have too many to eat raw or they are slightly past their peak, baking is an excellent alternative.

MAKES 8 SERVINGS

8 large peaches
½ cup apricot jam
2 tablespoons lemon zest
1 tablespoon lemon juice
2 tablespoons sugar

Preheat the oven to 375°F. Cut the peaches in half, remove the pits, and place the halves cut-side up in a shallow baking dish.

In a small bowl, whisk together the jam, 1 cup water, and lemon zest and juice. Spoon the mixture over the peach halves and lightly sprinkle with the sugar.

Bake for 30 to 45 minutes, until the peaches are very tender. Very ripe peaches will cook faster. Check several times during the baking and baste them with their juices. Serve with the juices drizzled over the top.

VARIATION:
- Substitute a drizzle of honey over each peach for the apricot jam.

Fruit Crumble

Crumbles and crisps—a deep layer of fruits baked under a crunchy topping—are great ways to make a simple dessert with an abundance of ripe fruits. Every season has delicious fruit options: stone fruits and berries in the summer, apples and pears in the fall and winter, rhubarb and strawberries in the spring. Feel free to mix fruits and berries in any combinations you like. I prefer a topping made with the healthy alternative of rolled oats in place of chopped nuts (especially when allergies are a concern).

MAKES 8 SERVINGS

FOR THE TOPPING:
1 cup rolled oats
⅔ cup flour
⅔ cup brown sugar
¼ teaspoon ground cinnamon (optional)
1 cup cold butter, cut in small pieces

FOR THE FILLING:
4 to 5 pounds ripe nectarines or peaches
1 tablespoon sugar, as needed

Combine the oats, flour, brown sugar, and cinnamon (if using) in a bowl. Mix well, then add the butter. Work the butter into the mixture with your fingers, a pastry blender, or a stand mixer with a paddle attachment, just until the mixture comes together and has a crumbly texture. Chill until ready to use.

Cut the nectarines in half, remove the pits, and cut into ⅓-inch-thick slices. If using peaches, dip the whole fruits in boiling water for 10 to 15 seconds, then carefully slip off the skins before pitting and cutting into slices. If the fruit is very tart, sprinkle with a little sugar. There should be about 7 cups of fruit.

Preheat the oven to 375°F. Pile the fruits into a 2-quart shallow baking dish and cover with the oat topping. Bake for 40 to 55 minutes, until the crisp topping is golden brown and the fruit is bubbling in the dish.

VARIATIONS:
- Add berries such as blackberries, raspberries, or blueberries to taste, as available.
- Serve with 1 or 2 tablespoons cold heavy cream per plate or a small scoop of vanilla ice cream.

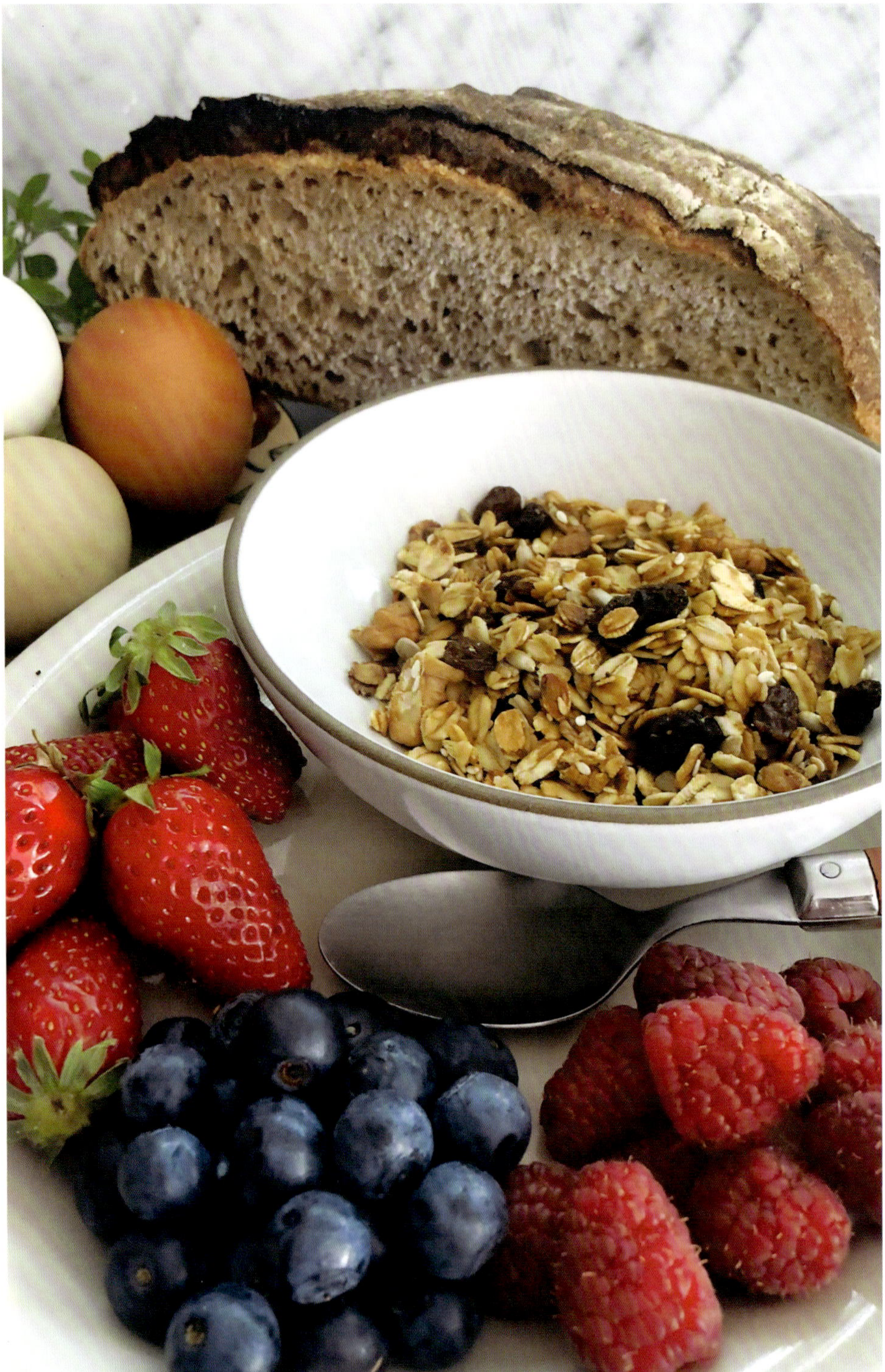

Breakfast

Kids need a nutritious, usually quick meal to start their day. We know that students who are hungry and undernourished cannot learn and perform well in school. Very young children are especially vulnerable developmentally to the effects of poor nutrition. Some states are now providing free school lunches and breakfasts for all students; the benefits are obvious and indisputable.

Whole grains and fresh fruits are a great way to start the day and give hungry kids the energy they need for a morning of classes. Porridge, granola, yogurt, buttermilk pancakes, and French toast are all delicious topped with fruits of all kinds or fruit compote.

Breakfast can be a way to maximize the efficiency and economy of home and school kitchens. In many cultures it's a combination of what might remain from the previous night's dinner and fresh bread, naan, tortillas, rice, or noodles. I love a savory breakfast rather than a sweet one. A go-to for me is a warm tortilla with beans, a little cheese, cumin, salt, and salad greens. Leftover rice and vegetables can make a quick and tasty fried rice in the morning. Extra bread slices turn into French toast, and overripe fruits can be made into a juicy compote.

Multigrain Porridge

This is a tasty version of rice porridge that my daughter taught me how to make. It is easy to put together with cooked brown rice and added grains for extra nutrition.
MAKES 1 QUART

¼ cup red quinoa
¼ cup millet
1 cup Brown Rice (page 73)
¼ cup raisins

¼ teaspoon kosher salt
Butter or milk (optional)
Maple syrup or honey

The night before, soak the quinoa and millet together in 2 cups water. When ready to cook, drain the quinoa and millet in a fine-mesh strainer and rinse well.

In a saucepan, combine the cooked rice, quinoa, millet, raisins, salt, and 3½ cups water. Bring to a boil, skim off any foam, and stir, making sure nothing sticks to the bottom or sides of the pan. Cover and simmer gently until the quinoa and millet are fully cooked and beginning to break down, 30 to 40 minutes. Stir frequently as it thickens, and cook until the porridge is the texture you like. Add water if it gets too thick. Serve with a little butter or milk, and maple syrup or honey for sweetness, if you like.

VARIATIONS:
- Serve with chopped nuts or any fresh fruits that you like, such as berries.
- In place of the raisins, add other dried fruits, such as cranberries, dates, cherries, or apples.
- For a savory porridge, omit the raisins and finish with butter and some chopped herbs or chives. Top with a soft-boiled or poached egg for a more substantial meal.

Oatmeal

Oatmeal for breakfast is almost too obvious to mention or detail in a recipe, but it remains a mainstay for good reason. Keep it fresh by varying the toppings, and serve immediately after cooking for a satisfying and nutritious start to the day.

MAKES 4 SERVINGS

4 cups water or low-fat milk
¼ teaspoon kosher salt
2 cups rolled oats

Butter or milk (optional)
Honey, maple syrup, or brown sugar (optional)

In a saucepan, bring the water or milk (or a combination) and salt to a boil. Stir in the rolled oats and lower the heat. Cook gently, stirring frequently, until cooked through and thickened to your liking, 5 to 10 minutes. Serve with a little butter and honey for sweetness, if you like.

VARIATIONS:
- Cook raisins or other dried fruits along with the oats.
- Serve with fresh fruits in any combination, or a cooked fruit compote. Add chopped nuts and a dollop of yogurt, if you like.

Granola

I prefer granola that does not have a lot of flavorings. This is a basic recipe that can be adjusted to your taste. Some people like to add cinnamon, cardamom, maple syrup, vanilla, or coconut—feel free to make it your way. Serve it with any combination of fresh fruits and milk, or a dollop of yogurt, if you like.

MAKES 1¾ QUARTS

4 cups rolled oats
¼ cup sesame seeds
½ cup sunflower seeds
½ teaspoon kosher salt
½ cup almonds
½ cup walnuts, coarsely chopped
⅓ cup neutral oil
⅓ cup honey
1 cup raisins (optional)

Preheat the oven to 350°F.

On a baking sheet, combine the oats, seeds, salt, and nuts. Drizzle over the oil and honey, mix well, and spread evenly over the sheet. Bake for 10 minutes, remove from the oven, stir, and spread the granola over the pan again. Repeat the stirring every 5 minutes or so for even cooking and to prevent over-browning at the edges. Bake until the granola is nicely toasted and golden brown, 30 to 40 minutes total. Remove from the oven and stir in the raisins (if using). Let cool completely before storing in jars or airtight containers.

VARIATIONS:
- Add other grains and seeds to the mix: ½ cup buckwheat groats, ½ cup red quinoa, ½ cup ground chia seeds.
- Add any other dried fruits along with the raisins.

Buttermilk Pancakes

These are delicious, light and fluffy pancakes. Serve with warm fruit compote and perhaps yogurt as an alternative to maple syrup.

MAKES 4 TO 6 SERVINGS

1½ cups whole wheat pastry flour	3 eggs
1 teaspoon baking powder	2 cups buttermilk
1 teaspoon baking soda	6 tablespoons butter, melted
1 teaspoon kosher salt	

Mix the flour and other dry ingredients in a large bowl.

Separate the eggs. Mix the egg yolks and buttermilk in a small bowl. Make a well in the flour mixture, pour in the buttermilk mixture, and stir until just combined. Add the melted butter and stir well.

In another bowl, beat the egg whites until they form soft peaks, then fold into the batter. If the batter is too thick, add more buttermilk.

Spoon the batter onto a hot buttered griddle and cook 2 to 3 minutes until the pancakes are golden brown on one side. Turn them over and cook until just done.

VARIATIONS:
- For the buttermilk, substitute a mixture of yogurt and milk. Or make the pancakes with regular milk: use 1½ cups milk, omit the baking soda, and use 2 teaspoons baking powder instead.
- For half the flour, substitute a mixture of other whole-grain flours: spelt, cornmeal, rye, oat, or buckwheat.

French Toast

This is a good way to make a delicious meal from day-old bread. Serve with any number of fruit toppings, such as warm applesauce, macerated berries, fruit compote, or bananas and yogurt.

MAKES 4 SERVINGS

2 eggs
½ teaspoon kosher salt
⅔ to 1 cup milk
½ teaspoon vanilla extract (optional)
8 slices whole-grain bread
Butter, for the griddle

Beat the eggs together and mix in the salt, milk, and vanilla (if using). Dip the bread slices into the mixture and cook on a hot buttered griddle until nicely browned on each side. Serve hot with the toppings of your choice.

Quesadillas

Kids love quesadillas, for breakfast, lunch, an after-school snack, or anytime.
MAKES 4 SERVINGS

1 cup grated Monterey Jack cheese
8 corn or whole wheat flour tortillas
1 tablespoon butter or oil

Sprinkle the cheese over 4 of the tortillas and then top with the remaining 4 tortillas. Heat a heavy skillet over medium heat. Add a bit of butter to the pan and put in a quesadilla, or more than one if the pan allows. Cook until golden, turn over, and cook on the other side until golden and the cheese is melted. Repeat with the remaining butter and quesadillas. Serve right away or hold in a warm oven while cooking the other quesadillas.

VARIATIONS:
- Add a scattering of thin slices of seeded jalapeño chiles and scallion and cilantro leaves. If squash blossoms are available, cut off the base to remove the anther or pistil, gently pull apart the brilliant flower petals, and lay them on the cheese.
- Use a mandoline to cut paper-thin slices of zucchini, salt them, and lay them over the cheese.
- Serve with fresh tomato or tomatillo salsa for dipping.
- For a more substantial plate, serve with warm beans, scrambled eggs, and salsa.

Potato Frittata

A frittata is a flat omelet, better at room temperature than just-cooked, which makes it a versatile dish for breakfast or lunch on the go, a picnic, or prepared for the next day. It is delicious on top of garlic toast. Add a drizzle of hot sauce or salsa if you like it spicy.

MAKES ONE 10-INCH FRITTATA

3 or 4 medium Yukon Gold potatoes (about 1 pound)
Kosher salt and fresh-ground black pepper
1 onion
4 or 5 garlic cloves
4 tablespoons plus 1 teaspoon olive oil
6 eggs
1 tablespoon chopped fresh marjoram leaves
2 tablespoons chopped chives

Peel the potatoes, cut in half lengthwise, and slice thin. Cook in boiling salted water, or steam, until just tender but not falling apart. Drain and cool.

Peel the onion and slice thin. Peel the garlic cloves and slice thin. Heat a sauté pan over medium heat, then add 2 tablespoons olive oil and the sliced onion. Cook gently, stirring occasionally, until tender and translucent, about 10 minutes. Add the garlic and continue cooking a few minutes, until soft and fragrant. Turn off the heat and let cool.

Break the eggs into a large bowl. Season generously with the salt and pepper, add the chopped herbs, and beat gently. Add the onion, garlic, and potatoes and mix gently.

Thoroughly preheat a 10-inch heavy or nonstick skillet over medium-low heat. Pour in 2 tablespoons olive oil, wait a few seconds, then pour in the egg-potato mixture. As the eggs set on the bottom, lift the edges to allow the uncooked egg to flow underneath. Continue to cook 5 to 10 minutes until mostly set. Invert a plate on top of the pan; carefully turn the plate and pan upside down to turn out the frittata onto the plate.

Return the pan to the heat, add the remaining 1 teaspoon olive oil, and slide the frittata back into the pan. Cook for 2 to 3 minutes, until just set. Slide the frittata onto a plate and serve warm or at room temperature.

VARIATIONS:

- Cut the potatoes slightly smaller, and cook the egg-potato mixture in lined muffin tins for individually portioned frittatas.
- Alternatively, cook the frittata in a 350°F oven, as long as the pan is ovenproof. Start the cooking on top of the stove, as described. After a few minutes, put the pan in the oven and cook until the frittata is set on top, 7 to 10 minutes.
- For a larger quantity, double the recipe, line a half hotel pan with parchment paper on the bottom and sides of the pan, and lightly oil the paper. Pour the egg mixture into the pan and bake for 40 to 45 minutes, until cooked through.
- In place of the potatoes, use other cooked vegetables such as peas, roasted squash or cauliflower, or wilted spinach, chard, or kale.

Hard-Cooked Eggs

I hear from school kitchen cooks that sometimes all their kids have time to eat in the morning before classes begin is a quick bite of egg and a piece of fruit. A good farm egg is an excellent source of protein to keep them going until lunchtime.

This is a method for cooking eggs so that their yolks will be just set and golden and moist in the center. Let the eggs come to room temperature. Put them in a pot and cover with water. Bring to a boil, adjust the temperature so the water just simmers, and cook for 5 minutes. Pour off the hot water and fill the pot with cold water. Crack the eggs all over when they are cool enough to handle, and peel off the shells.

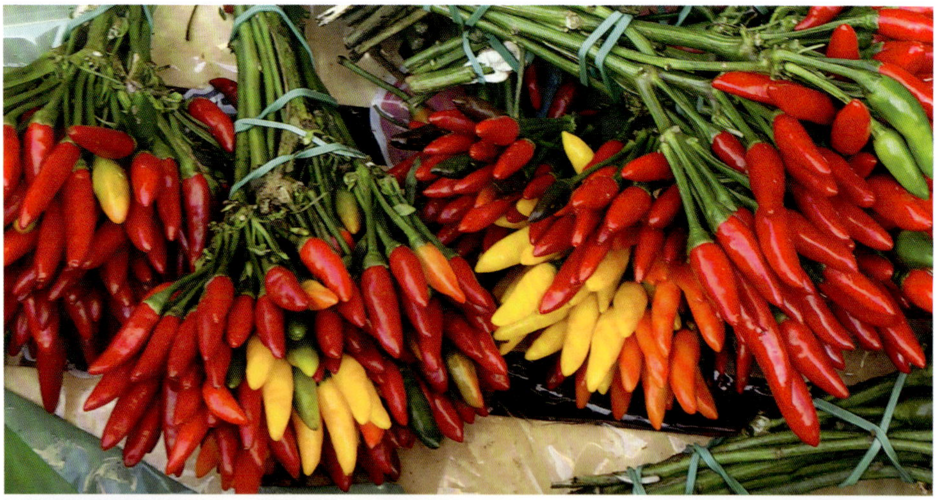
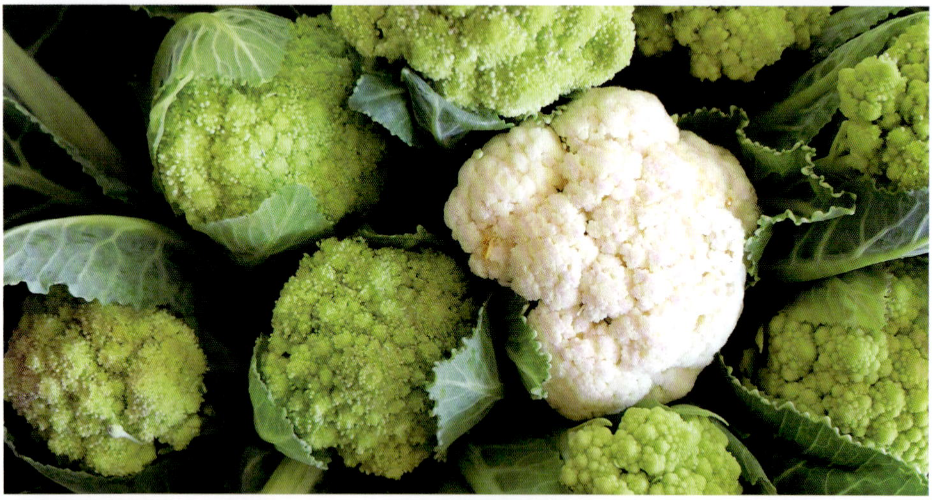
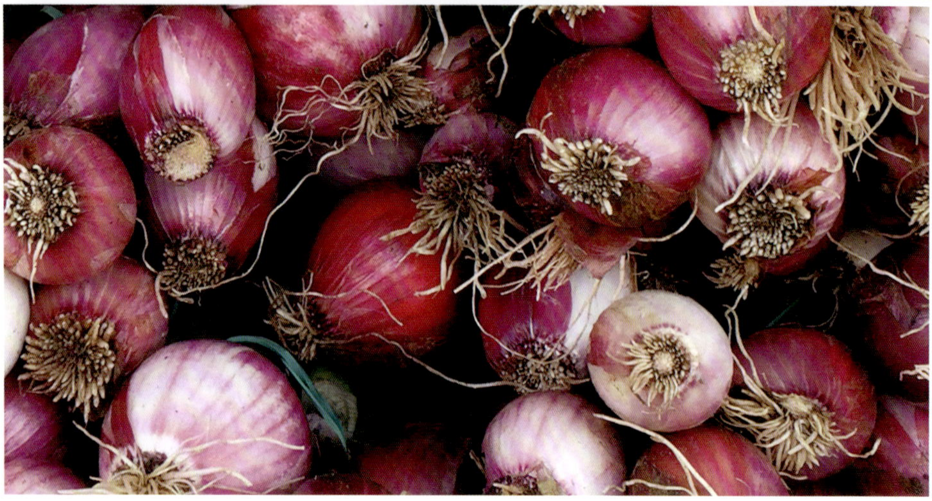

Pickles and Preserves

Pickling and preserving are not just for saving perishable seasonal abundance for long-term storage, such as tomatoes, but also methods of capturing and enhancing peak freshness to enjoy in the near term. Quick pickling preserves the bright crunch and color of all kinds of vegetables, to be eaten right away alongside a sandwich or salad or sealed in jars and stored for months to come. Fermented pickles are made utilizing the age-old method of lacto-fermentation, a simple process using salt and the naturally occurring bacteria found in the vegetables and the air. The salt prevents the growth of harmful bacteria and encourages beneficial microbes that convert the natural sugars of the vegetables to lactic acid. The acid preserves the vegetables and provides the sour taste to the pickles. The probiotic bacteria are hugely beneficial of our health.

Canned tomatoes are a treasure to have in the pantry, useful for so many dishes all year long. The ones you can yourself using fresh tomatoes at their peak of ripeness and flavor are going to be better than any you buy in a tin can. Process jars packed with raw tomatoes in a water bath or, if space allows, freeze to preserve the freshest flavor.

Dried fruit is universally loved by kids. It can be expensive to buy, but drying in a simple dehydrator is an easy and economical alternative. Once dried, the fruit keeps up to a year or more without refrigeration, if the kids don't get to it first.

Quick Pickles

Fresh pickles, as opposed to fermented, are cooked quickly in spicy vinegar brine until just tender but still a bit crisp. Many vegetables are good for pickling; prepare as many as you like, but cook them separately to control the texture.

1½ cups white wine vinegar or cider vinegar
2½ tablespoons sugar
1 teaspoon kosher salt
1 bay leaf
2 or 3 thyme sprigs
½ teaspoon coriander seeds
2 whole cloves
1 dried cayenne pepper or a pinch of dried red chile flakes
Assorted vegetables, such as carrots, fennel, turnips, cauliflower and broccoli florets, onions, green beans, okra, beets

Combine the vinegar, 1½ cups water, sugar, salt, bay leaf, thyme, coriander, cloves, and pepper in a nonreactive saucepan, bring to a boil, then reduce the heat to a simmer. Prepare the assorted vegetables by peeling, if needed, trimming, and cutting them into same-size shapes—whole or halved small carrots, sliced large carrots, sliced fennel, quartered small turnips, quartered small onions, sliced beets. Because cooking times will vary, cook the different vegetables separately in the simmering brine. Scoop them out when they are just cooked through but still a little crisp. Let cool and drain. Once all the vegetables are cooked, combine and serve at room temperature, or chill. If you like, pack the vegetables in jars, cover with the cool pickle brine, and refrigerate for up to 1 month.

A similar method for especially tender young vegetables such as carrots, radishes, fennel, and turnips is to macerate, not cook, them in the brine. Heat the brine to boiling, then let it cool to room temperature. Soak the vegetables separately for 30 to 60 minutes, until they are flavored through but still retain their crunchy freshness. Drain, then chill to further crisp and refresh them.

Pickled Red Cabbage

I love bright pickled red cabbage on tacos and sandwiches, particularly a falafel, flatbread, and raita sandwich.

MAKES 1½ TO 2 QUARTS

½ head red cabbage (about 1 pound)
1¼ cups cider vinegar
2 teaspoons sugar
1½ teaspoons kosher salt
2 garlic cloves, peeled and sliced (optional)
2 teaspoons coriander seeds
A few black peppercorns

Core and shred the cabbage with a knife or a mandoline and put the shreds in a large heatproof bowl. Combine the vinegar, 1¼ cups water, sugar, salt, garlic (if using), coriander, and peppercorns in a saucepan and heat to a simmer. Pour the hot brine over the cabbage and toss lightly. Let the cabbage sit for 1 to 2 hours. If not serving right away, pack the cabbage in jars and refrigerate for up to 1 week. The flavor will intensify as it sits.

Dill Pickles

MAKES 3 QUARTS

FOR THE PICKLES:
25 to 30 pickling cucumbers, 3 to 4 inches long (about 10 pounds)
2 cups white wine vinegar (7% acidity)
6 tablespoons kosher salt

FOR EACH JAR:
½ teaspoon black peppercorns
½ teaspoon coriander seeds
2 bay leaves
2 fresh dill flower heads (or 1 tablespoon dill seeds)
1 small dried chile
2 garlic cloves, peeled

Wash the cucumbers well, making sure to remove any blossoms remaining on the ends; they contain an enzyme that can make the pickles mushy.

Wash and sterilize three 1-quart canning jars with lids for 5 minutes in boiling water. Combine the vinegar, salt, and 1¼ cups water in a saucepan and heat to a simmer.

Measure the spices and flavorings into each warm jar and pack the cucumbers into the jars. Fill with simmering brine to within ¼ inch of the top, wipe the rims dry, and seal with the lids and bands. Store in a cool, dark place for at least 1 month (the flavor is better after 2 or 3 months) to allow to cure before eating. Refrigerate any jars that fail to make a tight seal. The pickles will keep for a year or more. Refrigerate after opening.

Fermented Pickles

You can make crunchy, colorful pickles with many vegetables—green beans, carrots, fennel, turnips, kohlrabi, cauliflower florets, asparagus, cucumbers, okra, daikon radishes, watermelon radishes, and other radishes. They are not only delicious but a great source of probiotics for a healthy gut biome.

It is most helpful to use glass weights that fit inside the tops of the jars to keep the vegetables under the surface during fermenting. And use fermenting lids for the jars, which are designed to allow air bubbles to escape so that the jars don't overflow. These supplies and more can be found in shops that sell preserving supplies or online.

MAKES 2 QUARTS

6 to 7 cups cut vegetables
Optional flavorings: garlic cloves, sprigs of fresh herbs, dried chile flakes, crushed black peppercorns

2 tablespoons fine sea salt
2 quarts filtered water

Wash and prepare the vegetables of your choice. Leave small ones whole or cut into sticks, wedges, slices, or florets.

Wash and dry two 1-quart jars or one half-gallon jar. (If you have a fermenting vessel, all the better.) If using, divide the garlic cloves, herb sprigs, and chile flakes between the jars. Layer the vegetables in the jars, pressing down to fit in as many as you can, leaving 2 inches of headspace.

Add the salt to the filtered water (do not use chlorinated or tap water), stir to dissolve, and then pour over the vegetables until just barely covered. Slide a knife or thin spatula down the sides of the jars to release any air bubbles.

Use a glass weight to keep the vegetables under the brine, and cover the jar with a tight regular lid or an airlock fermenting lid. If you are using a regular lid, you will need to open the jar once a day to release the pressure. To be safe and avoid a spill, put the jars on a tray in case there is overflow.

Let the vegetables ferment at room temperature, about 70°F, for 4 to 5 days, until the flavor and texture are to your liking. When finished, remove the weight, replace the top with a regular lid, and refrigerate. The fermentation will nearly stop but the flavor will continue to develop. The brine may be a bit cloudy, which is fine. They will keep well in the refrigerator for 1 to 2 months.

Kimchi

Kimchi, the heart and soul of Korean cuisine, is exciting to make. Beautiful leafy cabbage and strong vibrant flavors are transformed by the magic of lacto-fermentation. It is a relatively quick two-day process, immediately rewarding. The kimchi is delicious and ready to eat freshly fermented but will keep indefinitely in the fridge. The flavor and texture will change and develop the longer it ages.

MAKES 2 QUARTS

FOR THE CABBAGE:
1 or 2 heads napa cabbage (about 3 pounds)
½ cup kosher salt

FOR THE RICE PASTE:
1 tablespoon rice flour
1 tablespoon brown sugar

FOR THE FISH PASTE:
1 small onion, peeled and quartered
2 garlic cloves, peeled
1-inch piece ginger, peeled
2 anchovies (or ¼ cup fermented salty fish)

FOR THE KIMCHI:
1 bunch scallions, sliced
1 cup julienned carrot
1 cup julienned Korean radish
1 bunch garlic chives, sliced (optional)
¼ cup fish sauce
¾ cup gochugaru (Korean chile flakes), or more to taste

Separate the cabbage into halves or quarters: Cut through the core, keeping the wedges intact, and pull apart the upper leaves. Massage the salt into the layers of the leaves. Drain in a colander for 2 hours, turning every 30 minutes. Rinse and drain the cabbage.

Make the rice paste: Cook ½ cup water and the flour over low heat for 10 minutes, then add the brown sugar and cook for 2 minutes more. Let cool.

Make the fish paste: Purée the onion, garlic, ginger, and anchovy in a food processor until smooth.

Make the kimchi: In a bowl, combine the rice paste, fish paste, scallions, carrot, radish, garlic chives (if using), fish sauce, and gochugaru and mix well. Spread the cabbage leaves with the flavorings and vegetables, press the leaves back together into the original wedge shape, and pack the wedges tightly into one half-gallon or two 1-quart jars sterilized for 5 minutes in boiling water or a sterilized fermenting vessel. As the cabbage releases juices, press down to keep it under the surface of the brine. If necessary, use a glass weight to keep it submerged. Cover loosely and ferment for 2 to 3 days, until the kimchi is the right sourness for your taste. Repack, if you prefer, and push the cabbage down under the liquid. Refrigerate.

Canned Tomatoes

Preserving tomatoes when they are ripe and abundant is one of the most useful annual tasks in stocking a pantry. These all-purpose preserved tomatoes don't have particular seasonings or aromatics, so they are versatile enough to be used in any recipe that calls for canned tomatoes. I prefer fleshy, paste-style tomatoes, such as San Marzano and Amish Paste, to make sauce with natural richness and viscosity. Other, juicier varieties, such as Early Girl, result in preserved tomatoes that are more liquid, most useful in soups and stews rather than sauces. Whichever variety you choose, make sure you have ripe, flavorful, sound tomatoes.

MAKES 8 QUARTS

14 pounds tomatoes
8 teaspoons kosher salt
1 teaspoon citric acid

Prepare the jars: Wash eight 1-quart canning jars, lids, and bands, and sterilize for 5 minutes in boiling water. Reserve the jars, lids, and bands on a clean towel.

Wash the tomatoes, discarding any that have rotten spots or significant blemishes. Bring a large pot of water to boil and blanch the tomatoes in small batches for 15 to 30 seconds, then remove and cool in a large bowl of cold water. Once cool, slip off the skins and cut out the stems. Cut the tomatoes into chunks and put them into a large, heavy-bottomed pot. Cook over medium heat until they begin to break down and just come to a simmer, then cook for 2 minutes more, stirring occasionally. You may need to simmer the tomatoes in a few batches. Add 1 teaspoon kosher salt and ⅛ teaspoon citric acid to each jar, and while the tomatoes are still hot, pack them into the quart jars, leaving ½ to ¼ inch of headspace.

Wipe the rims clean, place the lids on the jars, and screw on the bands (not too tight). In a large canning kettle or water bath pot, heat (but not to boiling) enough water to cover the tops of the jars by 1 to 2 inches. Lower the jars into the pot, bring the water to a boil, and process at a gentle boil for 40 minutes. Remove the jars from the water and allow to cool completely before moving and storing. As the jars cool, you will hear the pop of the lids sucking down and creating an airtight vacuum seal to protect the contents in the jars. If a jar fails to seal, and there is an air bubble remaining at the center of the lid, refrigerate until ready to use. The tomatoes will keep in cool, dark storage for at least a year.

VARIATIONS:
- Make tomato sauce, fully cooked and flavored as you like, and process in the same way.
- Alternatively, sterilize clean jars by heating them in a 250°F oven for 20 minutes or so, until ready to fill and process.

Tomato Confit

Confit refers to the French method of cooking something in oil, fat, or syrup as a way of preserving it. Cooking tomatoes this way intensifies and concentrates their flavor; each one is silky, tender, and sweet.

MAKES 6 SERVINGS

6 firm ripe tomatoes
A few sprigs basil
Kosher salt

6 to 8 garlic cloves, peeled (optional)
¾ cup olive oil

Preheat the oven to 350°F.

Peel and core the tomatoes. Scatter the basil in the bottom of a baking dish just large enough to hold the tomatoes snugly. Arrange the tomatoes stem-side down on top of the basil. Sprinkle with the salt and add the garlic (if using) and olive oil.

Bake for about 50 minutes, basting occasionally with the oil and juices. The tomatoes are done when lightly browned and completely tender but not falling apart. Remove from the oven and let cool.

Serve at room temperature. The oil left behind can be used for a vinaigrette or added to another sauce or dish. If not using right away, refrigerate, freeze, or can the tomatoes with their juices and the oil.

Dried Fruits

At times, when you're blessed with an abundance of ripe fruits, there is only so much you can serve and eat fresh. Preserving it in some way becomes imperative. Drying, or dehydrating, is a good choice. Dried fruits are naturally sweet and delicious, so no added sugar is needed.

Traditionally, fruits are dried on screens in the sun. This is a possibility, of course, given the right conditions and context, but it's impractical for most people and kitchens. Solar dehydrator plans are available online and are fairly easy to make. The most reliable way is to use a food dehydrator made specifically for drying produce on screen shelves, with easy-to-control, low temperatures and a timer.

Choose fruit to dry that is unblemished and perfectly ripe but not soft. Wash and dry well before starting. Cut the fruit into same-size pieces so they will dry evenly. Slice pears, apples, persimmons, even mandarins into ¼-inch slices. Remove any seeds. Cut other stone fruits in half and remove the pits. Apricots, figs, and plums can be dried in halves, cut-side up, while nectarines and peaches do better cut in ⅓-inch wedges. Peaches may need to be peeled before drying: Dip them in boiling water and then directly into cold. The skins will slip off.

Some fruits, such as apricots, peaches, and nectarines, will oxidize and brown while drying. If you prefer to prevent browning, prepare a solution of ascorbic acid and water (½ teaspoon ascorbic acid to 1 quart water), and submerge the cut fruit in the solution for no longer than 5 minutes before drying.

Lay out the pieces of cut fruit on drying trays in a single layer without them touching each other. Dry at 130° to 135°F. Fruits vary in moisture content, so check the fruits from time to time during the process. Start checking thinly sliced fruits such as apples after 8 hours; juicier fruits may take much longer. Cool the fruits for a few minutes before testing for doneness. Cut it in half to see if it has dried all the way through. Properly dried fruit should be pliable and no longer tacky. If it is moist or sticky, it needs longer drying. Be careful not to overdry the fruit or it may become unpleasantly brittle. Let it cool completely before storing, to avoid mold. Store in airtight containers in a dark, cool, dry place for up to 1 year.

Another method of drying and preserving fruit (and many other foods) is to freeze-dry it. Specialized equipment is required and can be expensive; however, there are significant advantages. Freeze-drying removes all the moisture through subzero temperatures, which leaves the fruit completely shelf-stable if stored in vacuum-packed containers or bags. The freeze-dried fruit is light and crunchy and usually retains its color and flavor. Cut whole fruits into halves, slices, or small pieces before freeze-drying. Small fruits such as berries, cherries, or grapes can be freeze-dried whole.

Frozen Berries

Freezing, if space allows, is a good way to preserve fragile and perishable berries. Wash the berries, spread them out on towels, and allow to completely air-dry. Hull strawberries and stem any other berries that need it. Spread the dry berries out on sheet trays so that they are not touching. Freeze for 1 to 2 hours, until the berries are completely firm.

Place the berries in airtight containers or ziplock bags, removing as much air as possible, and store in the freezer. (Always label and date freezer items.) They will keep for 1 month or so; after that they may crystallize with freezer burn. One way to avoid that and preserve the berries longer is to vacuum-seal them, which removes the air and moisture from the package. The berries should keep 6 months or more when properly sealed.

Other fruits, such as apricots, plums, and other stone fruits, pitted and cut in halves or wedges, can be frozen in the same way. They are delicious added to a bowl of porridge or oatmeal.

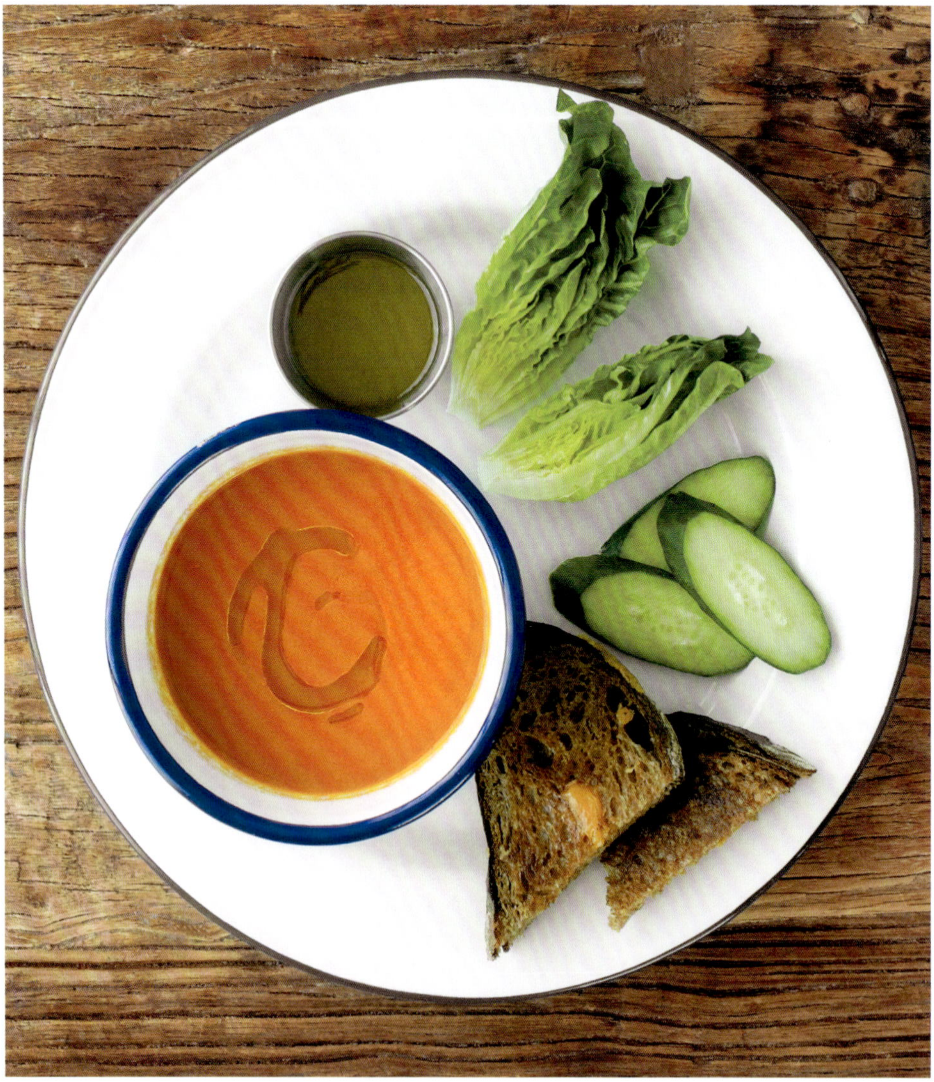

Seasonal Menus

Seasonality is the primary and most important consideration in conceiving and planning menus. It is simply not possible to eat ripe, delicious food consistently unless it has been grown locally and picked when it's in season. I find that cooking seasonally is both liberating and reassuring: it is not a loss when the fruits of summer fade, because of the anticipation of the apples, persimmons, and pears of autumn. In fact, cooking seasonally makes it *easier* to plan meals, not harder; it gifts you with a framework of what's available, delicious, and affordable at any time of the year. Find the ingredients that are in season near you, put them at the center of the menu, and build out from there.

The *how-to* methods of the Menu Staples recipes are the building blocks—salads, and dressings, brothy and puréed vegetable soups, beans and rice, braised meats, roasted vegetables, pasta and sauces, fresh fruits. The *what* to cook depends on the products of the moment: Are there carrots and beets to add to your salad, or cherry tomatoes and cucumbers? When the winter squashes arrive, it is time for golden butternut soup and roasted slices of delicata squash. In cooler months, bunches of shiny fresh chard and leafy greens can be sautéed with garlic, combined with white beans and pasta, or mixed with potatoes and eggs in a frittata. In summertime, sweet corn can be boiled on the cob, sautéed with chile and lime, or puréed into soup.

Seasonality cannot be strictly defined by the calendar, especially in the era of climate change. Many ingredients straddle the seasons—some cool-weather crops are very good in both fall and spring. And, of course, what ingredients and fresh produce are available will vary from region to region, but the principle of sourcing locally and following the seasons remains the same.

The menus that follow are just a few examples of planning seasonally and are meant to inspire and encourage you to fall in love with the rhythms of nature, wherever you live.

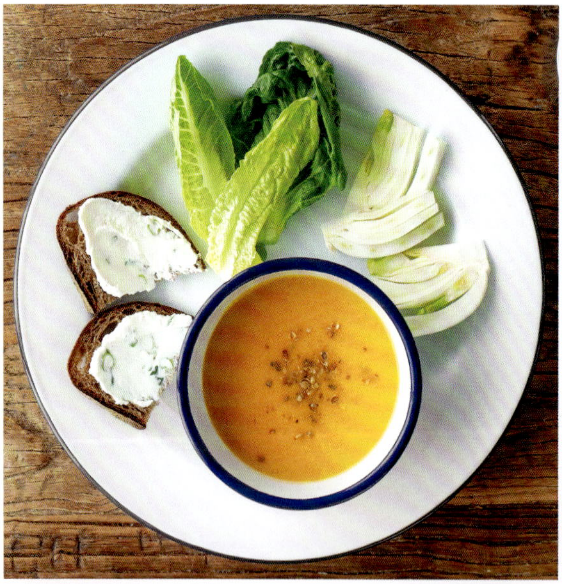
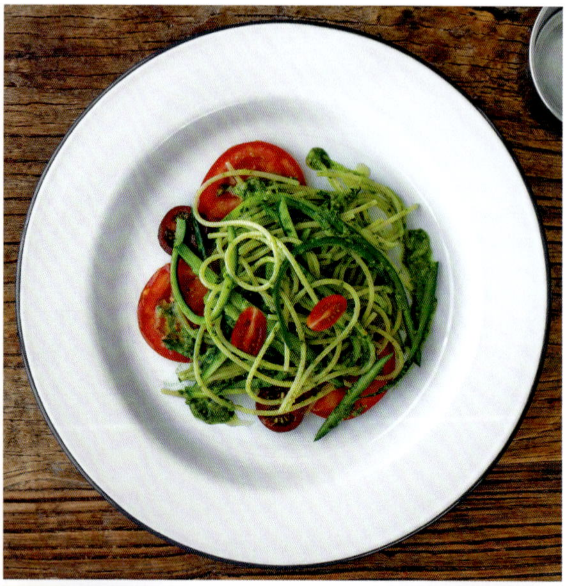
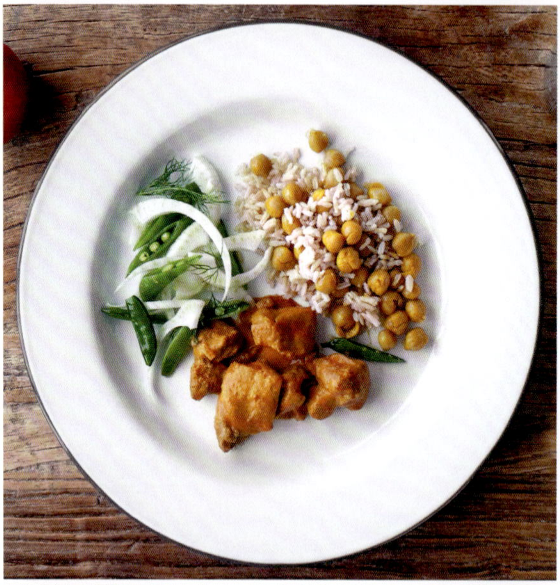
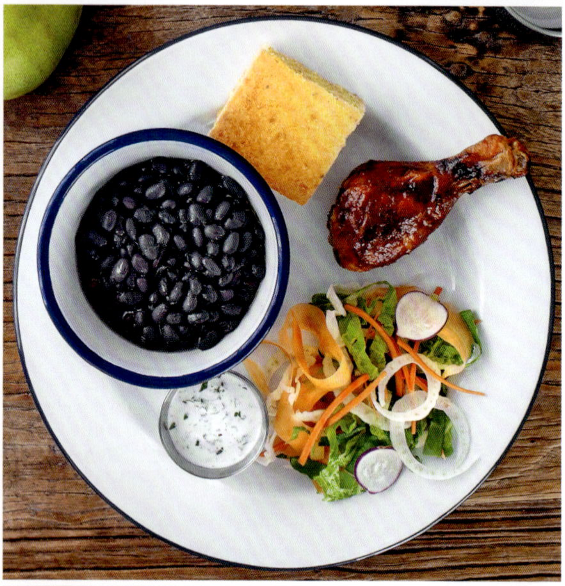
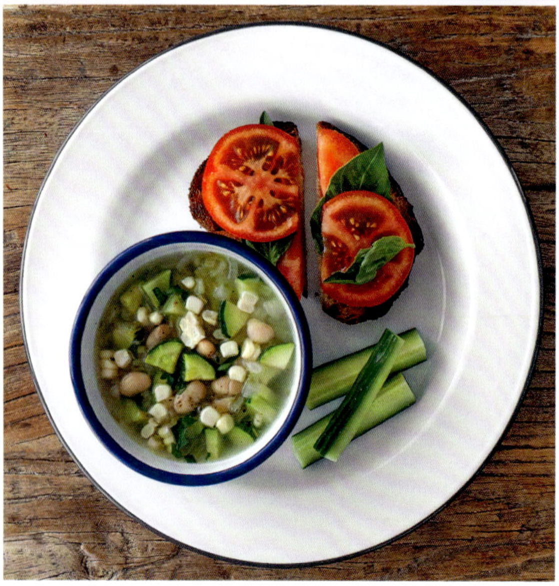
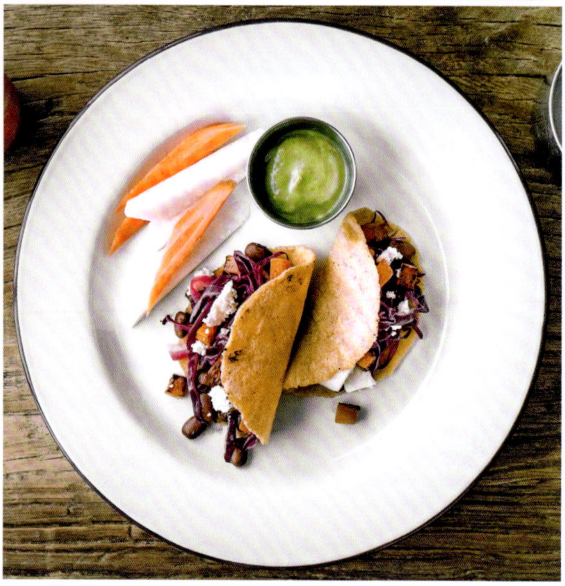

Summer / Fall

Pesto pasta with tomatoes and roasted zucchini

Tomatoes and aioli on focaccia, green salad,
and green beans with marjoram

Aioli plate with vegetables, eggs, tomatoes,
potatoes, and toasted bread

Quesadillas, sautéed corn with chile and lime,
and napa cabbage slaw

Chicken tomato curry, chickpeas and brown rice,
and fennel and snap pea salad

Butternut squash soup, herbed cheese toasts,
and shaved fennel salad

Barbecue chicken, black beans, cornbread,
and shaved vegetable salad

Focaccia ham and cheese sandwich with pickled vegetables

Roasted squash and pinto bean tacos with
avocado salsa, jicama, and carrots

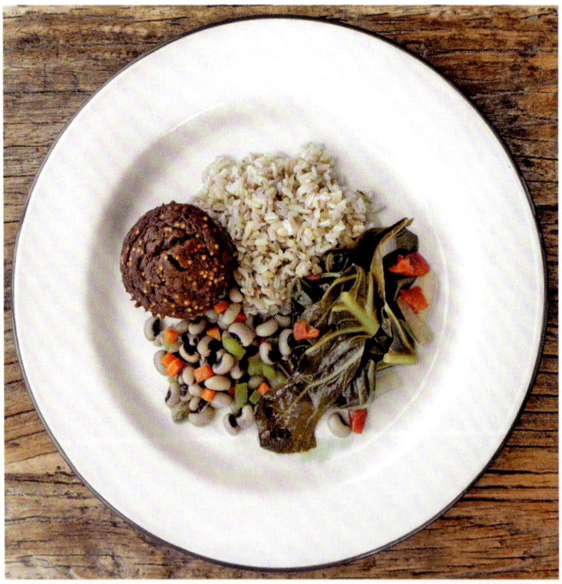

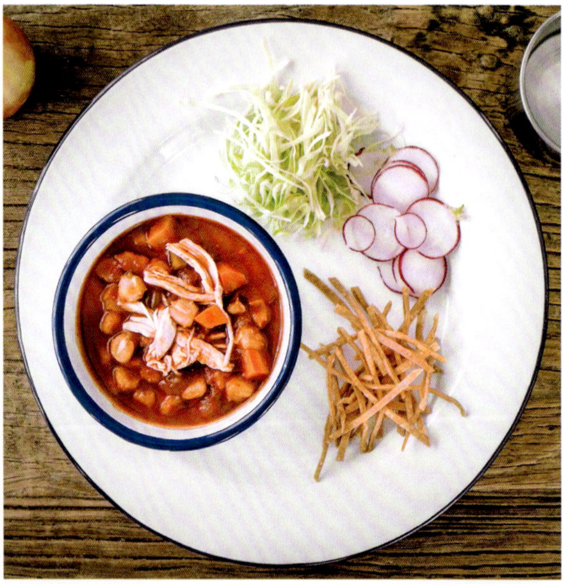

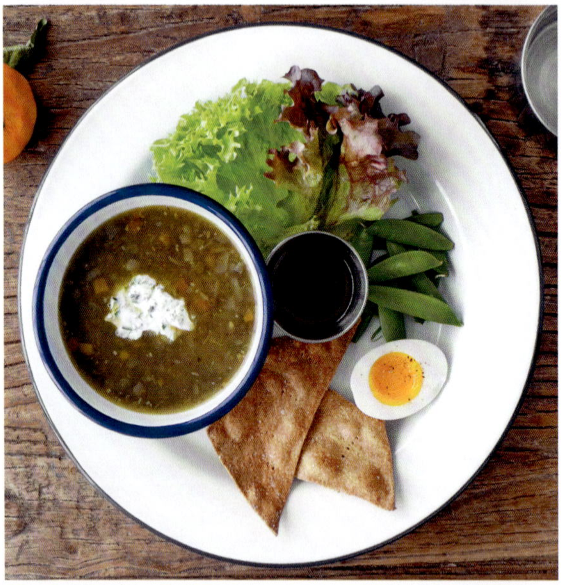

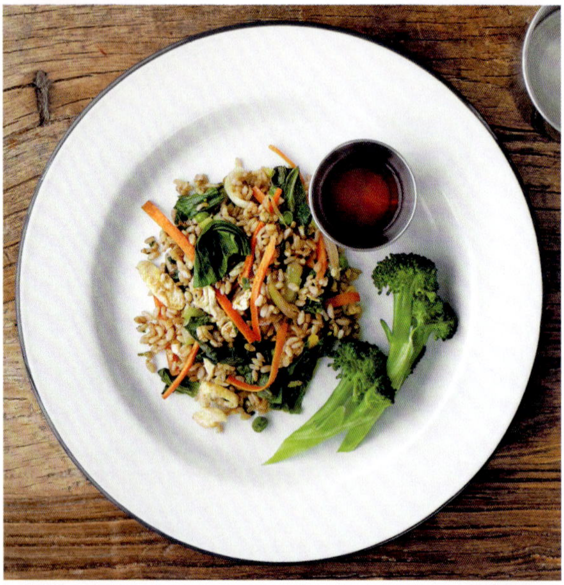

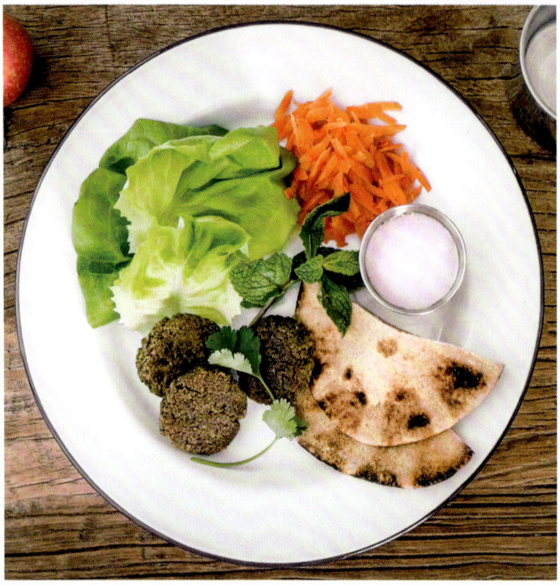

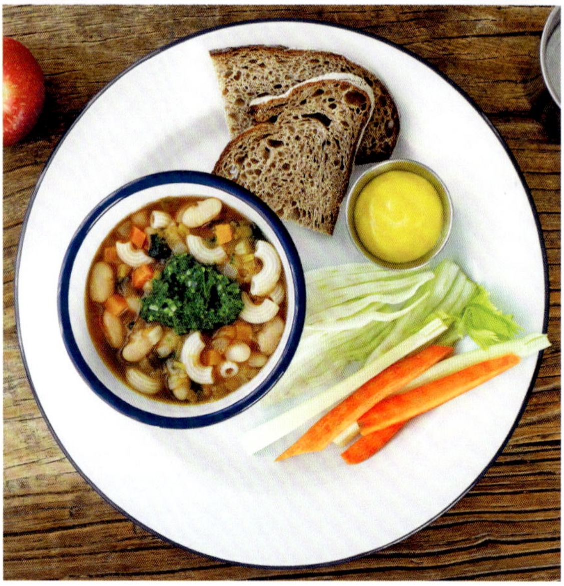

Fall / Winter

Minestrone with kale pesto, garlic toasts,
and aioli and vegetables

Vegetable fried rice, broccoli, and fall fruit cup

Polenta with meatballs, tomato sauce, and sautéed chard

Falafel and pickled red cabbage with pita bread,
raita, and carrot salad

Pozole with chicken, fried tortillas, radishes, and cabbage

Black-eyed peas with rice, collard greens, and a millet muffin

Roast chicken with salsa verde and
mashed potatoes and celery root

Green lentil soup, pita toasts, egg,
and salad vinaigrette

Potato and chard frittata with lettuce, vegetables,
and vinaigrette

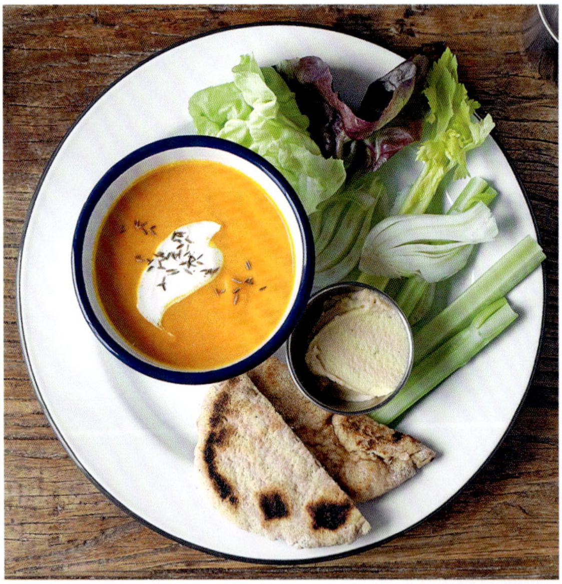
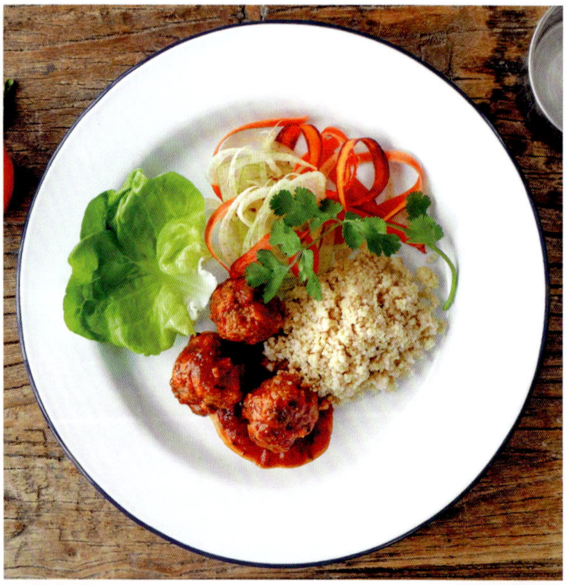
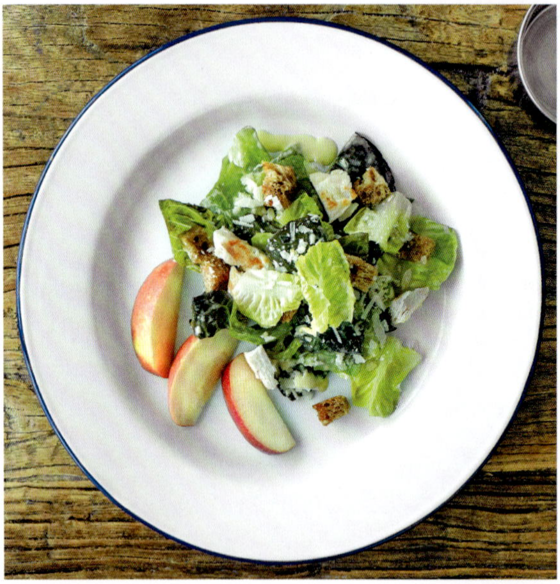
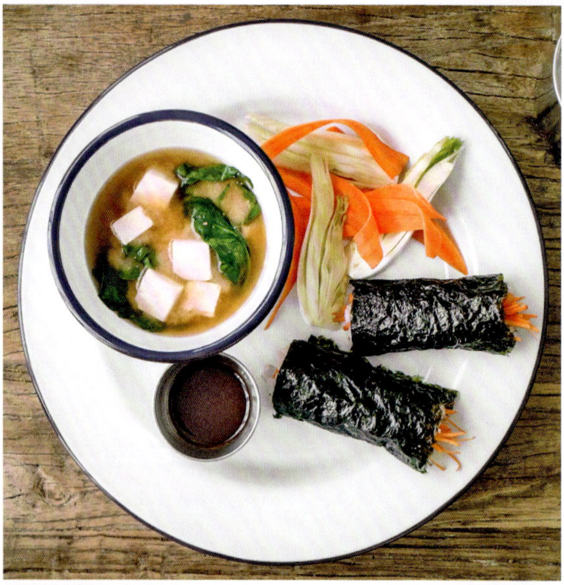
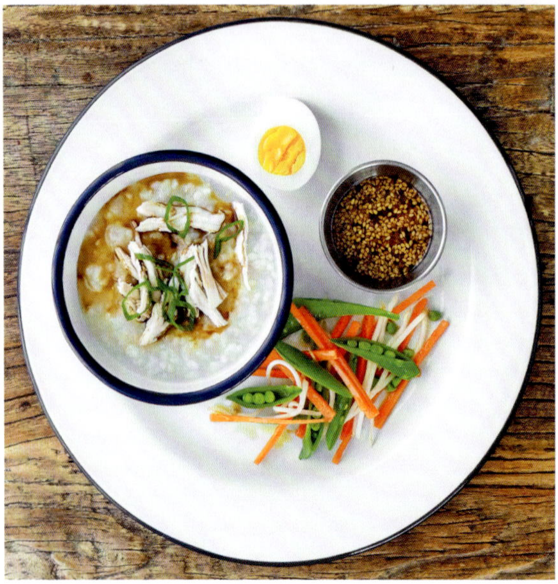
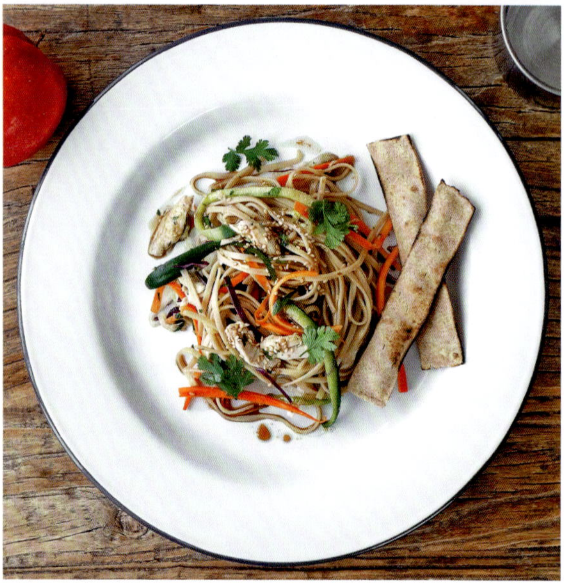

Spring / Summer

Carrot soup with pita bread, hummus, and spring vegetables

Rice noodle, chicken, and vegetable salad with crackers

Spicy lamb meatballs, couscous, and shaved vegetable salad

Carrot sushi, miso soup, vegetables, and tamari sauce

Chile pork tacos with tomato salsa, radishes,
and napa cabbage slaw

Focaccia pizza and Caesar salad

Corn soup, cheese and squash quesadilla, and cherry tomato
and cucumber salad

Chicken congee, baby bok choy, and soy-sesame dipping sauce

Hummus plate with crisp vegetables, romaine leaves,
olives, and crackers

Acknowledgments

My sincere thanks to the following people:

To Sylvia Osborne-Cailerno and Jeremy Scheiblauer for enthusiastically taking on the initial recipe and menu development and for working creatively within the constraints of nutritional and reimbursement guidelines. To Sylvie's twins, Salvador and Bella, child taste testers extraordinaire.

Thank you to longtime collaborator Patricia Curtan for writing, photographs, and design. To Cristina Mueller for patient wordsmithing and editing.

To photographer Don Hicks for beautifully capturing lunch on the plate.

I am most grateful to Steve Sullivan from Acme Bread Company for sharing bread recipes and for his continuous generous support of the Edible Schoolyard Project.

Thank you to willing recipe testers and contributors Nathan Alderson, Sharon Jones, Jeff Louie, Jennifer Sherman, and Jessica Washburn.

I want to express my appreciation and encouragement to all the dedicated professionals in school kitchens who care deeply about children and strive to serve them the good, healthy, and delicious food that they deserve.